DECORATING
YOUR FIRST
APARTMENT

DECORATING YOUR FIRST APARTMENT

Karen Fisher
Illustrated by Paul Wollman

Fawcett Columbine

New York

A Fawcett Columbine Book
Published by Ballantine Books
Copyright © 1986 by Karen Fisher
Illustrations copyright © 1986 by Paul Wollman

All rights reserved under International and
Pan-American Copyright Conventions.
Published in the United States by Ballantine
Books, a division of Random House, Inc.,
New York, and simultaneously in Canada by
Random House of Canada Limited, Toronto.

Library of Congress Catalog Card Number: 85-90592
ISBN: 0-449-90141-6

Cover design by Andrew Newman
Cover photo by Don Banks
Text design by Beth Tondreau
Manufactured in the United States of America

First Edition: October 1986
10 9 8 7 6 5 4 3 2 1

CONTENTS

My thanks to the spectacularly
talented designers who made this
book possible by giving so generously
of their wisdom, sensitivity, and
vision. I'm also very grateful for the
special wisdom and insights of my
editor, Joëlle Delbourgo. Special
thanks also to my agent, Barbara
Lowenstein, for her support of this
book from its inception.

DECORATING YOUR FIRST APARTMENT

INTRODUCTION

Whether you're on your own for the first time, about to share a new apartment with a friend, or starting over after years of being part of a couple, you're probably not sure where to begin when it comes to decorating your first apartment. It's one of those things that you don't think about until you're confronted with an empty apartment—or a cluttered one that you realize needs improving. Suddenly dozens of choices have to be made: how to select a color scheme, create a floorplan, or find the right sofa.

Decorating Your First Apartment has been designed to help you overcome these problems. This guide starts with the assumption that you want to decorate your studio or one-bedroom apartment tastefully—with the minimum amount of money in the shortest period of time and with the least amount of trauma. *Decorating Your First Apartment* is a handbook that will guide you through each of the decisions that you'll be making—and will show you how to enjoy the process of making a new home!

I've been the decorating editor for *Cosmopolitan*, *Esquire*, and *American Home* and have helped hundreds of people who are starting out. I know where the trouble spots are, and I'll help you avoid them. When you're buying paint, do you know whether to ask for latex or an oil base? Do you know the least expensive way to install track lights? Whether to buy a Murphy bed or a convertible sofa? These aren't things anyone is born knowing. Wherever possible, I've anticipated your questions. Instead of letting you worry about whether a sofa will be the right size for your room, I show you how to do a floorplan that will give you confidence in your choice. And throughout the book, I show dozens of different floorplans of rooms that are similar in size and proportion to yours.

The biggest problems in decorating are taste and money. Not a surprise, right? But just when you most need advice about style and keeping costs down, you often can least afford it. For this book, I've interviewed ten top decorators who plan the kinds of apartments you dream about. Ordinarily, their prices might be outside your range, but here, you'll be getting the advice they give to clients who are paying top dollar. I've asked them the questions you would ask, and in these pages you'll find their answers.

What separates the amateur decorator from the professional is the planning process. The professional always looks at the overall apartment and needs of his or her client and rarely starts a job until every detail is planned. The amateur can't wait to get started and buys each piece praying for the best. When you have professional help, you'll begin to see the importance of planning. You'll also learn how to balance aesthetics against practicality.

Developing a decorating plan is a

step-by-step process. Each chapter of *Decorating Your First Apartment* deals with a step in the decorating process. Some of the steps may seem unnecessary, and you may be tempted to skip a chapter. Don't do it! Each chapter is vital. As you go from chapter to chapter, you'll begin to see how logical decorating can be.

In Chapter 1, "Discover Your Decorating Style," you'll start with the most important element in your decorating job—you! This chapter is designed to help you clarify your taste as well as your needs. You'll see how fantasy can become reality, if you do your homework.

In Chapter 2, "Meet Your Decorators," you'll get a private view of each designer's apartment. You'll see how different each decorator's approach is—and you'll further appreciate the reasons for the questions in Chapter 1.

Many of the designers' places are similar in size to yours. In addition to seeing how professionals solve their decorating problems, I'll help you critique each approach as a possible direction for your own apartment. It's important that you begin picking out ideas that can be adapted, and this will be your starting point.

In Chapter 3, "Plan Your Budget," we'll take on the next big issue: cost. Most decorating books assume that you've come into an inheritance and that your major purchases will be valuable antiques and custom-made sofas. Not so here. My assumption is that you want to make the most of your income. However, the best ideas can take money to execute. You'll need to determine what you can afford to do when. Don't feel badly because you can't buy everything you'd like. Even millionaires have to set priorities, and that is what you will do here.

The surprise in shopping for home furnishings usually is not the cost of any particular item. In fact, this may be the best time in history to be furnishing a place because so many fine designs have been copied or adapted at affordable prices. The problem when you are starting from scratch, though, is that you need so much—rugs, sofa, mattress and box springs, etc. Luckily, almost any item in home furnishings is on sale at some time during the year. If you are willing to wait and shop carefully, you should be able to find most of your necessities at a discount. You can't have everything when you're on a budget, but you can usually have a few choice objects if you're a canny shopper.

The step beginners are most tempted to skip is spatial planning. The idea of drawing a floorplan might seem like a dismal waste of time to you, but in Chapter 4, "Plan Your Space," you'll see how essential a floorplan really is. Once you overcome the mental barrier against working out a floorplan on graph paper (don't worry—we'll show you how!), you will begin to get lots of new ideas and will want to try furniture in different parts of the room. After all, there's no rule that says the sofa must be against the wall. With a floorplan, you can see whether it wouldn't be more interesting to place it in the middle of the room or on a diagonal. An added bonus: the more you experiment with plans, the easier it will become to imagine how the furniture you see in the shop will look in your apartment.

The four key elements in any apartment are the walls, floors, window treatment, and lighting. First, in Chapters 5 through 8, we'll examine each of these elements in separate chapters. Then, you'll see how important it is that these elements be considered together. You shouldn't choose a wall color before you've decided on the floor treatment, or the lighting before you've determined the window treatments. When you start thinking of the total effect, you're thinking like a designer!

And finally, a note about storage space, which is often one of the most difficult problems in an apartment. Our spaces seem to shrink just as our lives expand. In Chapter 9, "Stretch Your Storage Space," we'll give you a warehouse full of storage ideas.

Decorating Your First Apartment has several special features I'd like to point out. The first is our "$avvy $hopper" guides, which will give you a better idea of how much your furnishings will cost and will show you how to buy wisely. You may be surprised at how far you can stretch a few dollars if you plan cleverly, and the $avvy $hopper guides will give you a starting point in estimating your costs. However, you may be able to find some items for less than the prices I've listed, and you'll find others that are more expensive.

We've also added special hot "Tips" from the designers in separate boxes, highlighting their professional advice. And we've set off "How-To" information in the same way so you can see at a glance if a particular approach may be right for you.

In addition, we've included "Decorating Dilemmas" throughout the book which will give you valuable insights into the planning process. Your decorators have planned apartments for people who have been in the same position you are—starting to decorate their apartments—and who had particular problems they needed to solve. Whether your own decorating dilemmas involve space, walls, floors, windows, lighting or storage space, you'll find yourself identifying with your compatriots and loving the unique solutions your decorators have worked out. Feel free to adapt any of these ideas for your own place—that's why they're here!

One of the great surprises of decorating is how exciting it can be, and how anxiety-producing. The initial euphoria of having a place of your own is often followed by the anxiety of not knowing where to start, the depression about costs, the despair over whether you have made the right choices. But then there's the joy of finding the perfect piece, the contentment of living in a beautiful setting, and the satisfaction of having all your possessions around you.

How you approach decorating reveals a great deal about your personality. By the time you've completed decorating your first apartment, you will have learned as much about your own values as about furniture design. This is a rare experience, and I hope you enjoy it to the fullest.

DISCOVER YOUR DECORATING STYLE

When you work with a decorator, you have a partner who cares as much about your apartment as you do. This is a luxury we don't normally have; even our best friends get bored when we can't decide between color schemes. Yet decorating takes thought. Decorators understand this and help you focus on the area where your needs and dreams meet. They ask the questions you might not have thought to ask yourself. They probe for the reasons behind your choices. They give you a chance to think through your options completely.

A designer's starting point is the client—his or her personality, lifestyle, taste, prejudices, needs, likes and dislikes. Most decorators will spend several hours finding out how a client feels about basics, such as whether you need blackout curtains in the bedroom, extra cabinets in the kitchen, a place for magazines in the bathroom, or a sleep sofa in the living room.

Questions like this are not glamorous, but they are as important as whether you like floral chintz or modern furniture.

Following are the questions that your decorators would ask you during an initial interview before starting your job. Think these questions through carefully, and make notes to yourself where you find points of particular interest. You'll probably be surprised by how much you'll learn about yourself and your needs.

By the time you've finished this chapter you will not have a total decorating plan, but you should be able to articulate what you would want a decorator to do. This is the first, crucial step to doing it yourself!

DECIDE ON YOUR TASTES

Everyone has a certain style when it comes to decorating, but it's surprisingly hard for most of us to articulate what this style is without help. Luckily, there are a couple of good ways to figure out what your tastes are.

First, go to your nearest newsstand and buy as many decorating magazines as you can. Without worrying about the cost of what you see, tear out the pages that appeal to you. Your choices will reveal a great deal. Do you always opt for the warm country living rooms with stripped pine furniture and cozy quilts? Or do you find yourself attracted to a cool, modern, spare look with lots of glass and chrome? Although you may feel that you can't afford the rooms that appeal to you, take a closer look. Analyze the pictures for affordable elements, such as wall color or furniture style. Almost every furniture style has been reproduced inexpensively, and a beautiful color needn't cost any more to paint onto the wall than off-white.

Second, indulge yourself in fantasies of the apartment of your dreams.

Pretend, for a moment, that you have all the money in the world. While some of the elements of your dream apartment will be beyond your reach, you'll be surprised at how close you can come to your ideal by using ingenuity.

Use the following questions to help you start planning your dream apartment.

• Do you prefer a traditional or modern feeling? Think here of whether you like heavy drapes, lots of patterns, and the "busy" feeling of traditional, or whether you're more comfortable with clean lines, fewer patterns, and a more open feeling.

Before you make a final decision, browse around in department stores and furniture stores that have model rooms. See whether you are drawn to heavy club chairs and sofas with traditional lines; or whether you like the sculptural quality of the contemporary and the functional, the snappy look of the so-called "high tech;" or the warmth of country pine. Follow your instincts in choosing a favorite style. Although you can always mix traditional and modern, it's nice to know which you are most comfortable with.

Think about whether you'd be happy living with or without color on the walls. Most traditional furnishings and fabrics are best against a background color, whereas many contemporary rooms are most successful when the backgrounds are neutral.

Consider whether you'll want lots of accessories and personal touches. The traditional look lends itself to dozens of framed snapshots on an end table, piles of magazines on the coffee table, and lots of bric-a-brac; but contemporary rooms tend to be at their best when they are sleek and neat.

• What type of artwork appeals to you? Would you prefer one outrageous avant garde painting as the focal point of a room rather than a grouping of old photographs and prints? Would you be daring enough to mount a bent bumper on a sculpture stand and present it as art? In many contemporary rooms, the furniture and colors are very plain in order to serve as a background for art; in traditional rooms, the art often blends in and there are many more pictures and accessories.

• Are flowers and plants an important part of decorating for you? Would you be willing to allot $5 per week for fresh flowers? What type of floral arrangements appeal most to you—a bunch of daisies, a mixture of spring flowers, a single lily? Have you ever bought the perfect vase for your favorite type of arrangement? Decide whether flowers are a luxury or a necessity, and then focus on how to make flowers affordable—for example, by buying a vase that will elegantly hold a single bud, or looking for planted flowers that will last for a couple of weeks.

• Does wall-to-wall carpeting conjure up delicious visions of walking barefoot? Or does it seem too modern and impersonal to you? Would you be happier instead with a few well-chosen rugs with interesting patterns? Have you ever really shopped for rugs? Can you tell the difference between a Romanian and a Turkish kilim? (If you can't, see Chapter 6.) Rugs can be as important in a room as artwork, but there's a staggering number of choices. It would be well worth your while to spend a Saturday browsing in rug departments to become more aware of the interesting options.

• Is there one piece of furniture you've always yearned for, such as a beautiful writing desk, a down-filled sofa, a brass or four-poster bed, a butler's table? Sometimes one great-looking piece is worth splurging on because it will give the whole room a focal point, allowing you to cut back your expenditures on the other furniture.

• Do you approach decorating as a joy or as a necessity? Are you looking forward to poking around antique shops and ferreting out the best buys in rugs? Or would it bother you if it took six months to find the perfect end table? Would you prefer to have this whole period behind you? Your attitude is an important part of the decorating process. This is the time to coinsider what decorating means to you emotionally, because this will have a great effect on your overall decorating plan.

CONSIDER YOUR LIFESTYLE

It's seductive to imagine that decorating your apartment will revolutionize your lifestyle, that now you'll start entertaining brilliantly or setting the table even when you're eating alone. But in truth this rarely happens. Mostly, we take our old habits with us.

Now it's time to be realistic about the way you live. Be completely honest as you answer the following questions. You need to assess the way you live now, not the way you wished you live. After all, you'll be happier in your new apartment if it fits your personality, habits, and needs.

• How much time do you actually spend at home? How do you use the apartment when you're there? Do you like to watch television? To entertain? If you love to read, listen to music or play Scrabble with a date, then you have a starting point for your decorating. Readers should have lots of bookcases, a comfortable reading chair, good lighting; music buffs should allot space for their equipment and place their furniture so they can get the most pleasure from their speakers; backgammon or bridge players should have a game table. Establish your needs, and then decorate around them.

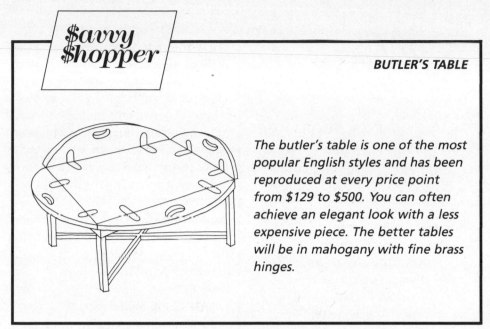

BUTLER'S TABLE

The butler's table is one of the most popular English styles and has been reproduced at every price point from $129 to $500. You can often achieve an elegant look with a less expensive piece. The better tables will be in mahogany with fine brass hinges.

• Are you neat? Do you automatically make the bed and hang up your clothes? If not, do you want new ways to organize your apartment so that there are places—such as cabinets, bookshelves, and additional drawers—to stash away the mess?

• Are you sentimental about your belongings? Do you save everything—clothes, old notebooks, souvenirs of a trip you took twelve years ago? Consider whether you need to keep absolutely all of this or whether you could weed out the most important belongings and find a place to save the other memorabilia until you get a larger place.

• Are you single and using the apartment as a background for seduction? What do you want the apartment to tell your dates about you?

• How do you feel about entertaining? Are you happy when friends drop by, or do you send out signals that it would be best if people called in advance? Are you comfortable whipping together a small dinner for a date or friends, or do you prefer to have parties catered? Do you enjoy cooking for a group, or would you prefer taking friends out to dinner? Are your parties casual or formal? Many people assume

they'll be entertaining and end up spending money on a dining room table that would be better spent on a sofa. If you are certain you'll entertain, then you should think about the number of people you'll be serving, whether you'll need extra seating for parties, etc.

• If you are living with another person, have you taken his or her needs into account? Have you allotted enough storage space and considered his or her taste in addition to yours? Do you think this relationship will be permanent enough for it to be feasible to share the decorating expenses, or should you buy most of the important pieces yourself so that the departure of a roommate won't mean the demolition of your apartment?

• Is it important that your apartment be a showplace that will impress friends and/or business associates? Sometimes an apartment is used to give others a signal—that you're successful, or that you can make a comfortable nest. If you want to project an image, you'll want to keep that goal in mind while you're decorating.

• Where do you usually eat when you're alone? At a restaurant? In the

living room? At the dining table? At the coffee table? Or at the kitchen counter?

• Are you a morning person or a night person? Morning people tend to like more light, airier colors, fewer window coverings. Night people tend to enjoy darker colors and more subtle lighting. Think about when you'll be using the apartment the most. If you go away almost every weekend, then you'll be spending most of your time in the apartment at night; if you enjoy puttering around the house on Saturday and having friends drop in for brunch on Sunday, then you'll want to decorate for those times.

• Do you spend a lot of time on the phone? Would it be a luxury or a necessity to have several extensions? Should you have a phone in the kitchen? The bathroom? If so, do you have tables for the extra phones, or should they be wall-hung? Do you want to rent or buy them? What style do you prefer? Messy phone cords are a consideration; so is convenience.

DETERMINE YOUR NEEDS

Here you should consider all the special needs that characterize your lifestyle.

• Do you have a pet? Should your upholstery and rugs be pet-proof?

• Do you have children, or do children often visit you? If so, you'll be happier with furnishings that will withstand a few crayon marks. You'll also need to think about where the children will eat, sleep, and play, and where their clothes and toys will be kept.

• What are your hobbies? Most hobbies take up as much space as they do time, and it's important to plan for them now.

• Do you have a collection to display? Even a few pieces of pottery or a dozen dolls, shells, or perfume bottles can be an interesting focal point for a room. Does your collection need a cabinet, shelf or special lighting?

• Do you meditate? Should a special place be provided for this?

• Do you exercise at home? Should space be allotted for exercise machines, bicycles, weights? Do you require special barres or mirrored areas?

• Do you need extra storage space for sports equipment, such as skis?

• Do you have a "green thumb"? Do you enjoy having lots of plants? Do you need special lighting for your plants?

• Do you play a musical instrument? Do you need to store it in a special place?

• Do you watch a lot of TV? In which room or rooms? Is it important to you that the TV be hidden from view when not in use?

• Do you work at home or bring papers home from the office? What kind of workspace will you need? File drawers? Bulletin boards? A desk? A typing table? Are you neat when you work? Should you have a rolltop desk rather than a writing table?

• Do you often have out-of-town guests? Do you need a convertible sofa in the living room?

• Do you enjoy having a bar area in the living room, or can you fix drinks in the kitchen?

• Do you put on makeup in the bedroom or in the bathroom? What kind of storage space do you need for your makeup, hair dryer, etc? Would you like a dressing table?

• Do you have a lot of clothes? Do you need extra-big closets? How do you like to store out-of-season clothes?

• Do you have a home computer? What kind of special space would you like for it?

EXERCISE EQUIPMENT

Once upon a time, only movie moguls could afford the luxury of private exercise centers. Now, however, sophisticated multipurpose equipment for home use often costs less than the price of a gym membership. In addition to the more expected weightlifting equipment and exercycles, you might also consider treadmills and rowing machines. When buying any machinery with a motor, be sure to check the warranty period. Expect to spend $300 and up.

ASSESS YOUR APARTMENT

Every apartment has both assets and limitations. A good decorating plan takes both into account. You may not be able to turn an apartment without a view into a sunny apartment that overlooks the river, but you can choose colors and window treatments that will show off the space you do have to its best advantage. Consider the following questions carefully. Your apartment is the most basic element of your decorating plan.

Think Ahead!

• How long do you plan to stay in the apartment? Will you move out as soon as you meet someone special or start making more money? If you are think- ing short-term, it's probably best to put the bulk of your investment into furniture rather than built-ins or improvements that will belong to the landlord when you move out. If you are thinking long-term, will you be staying long enough to amortize the cost of built-ins or permanent installations, such as wall-to-wall carpeting?

• If you paint the wall a color other than white, does your lease require painting it back when you move? Are you willing to do this?

• Does your lease allow you to choose the next tenant? If so, you may be able to sell improvements.

• Is the view worth playing up?

• What is the best feature of the apartment? The ceiling height? The layout? The size of the rooms? A fireplace? Is there one thing that you'd especially like to emphasize?

• Are the floors in good condition? Will they need refinishing? Do they need waxing?

• Are the walls in good condition? Should they be repaired and/or painted?

• Are plumbing or heating systems readily visible? Do you want to disguise them?

Living Room, Foyer, and Dining Area

• Do you avoid the living room because the furniture is too formal or there's not a comfortable place to read? Would you spend more time in the living room if you had a comfortable reading chair and good lighting?

• Is it advantageous to treat the living room and foyer as one space? Or does it work best when they visually appear to be two areas?

• Are the radiators bulky? Would you prefer a window treatment that covers them, such as vertical blinds or long curtains?

- Will the furnishings or rugs from your last place be temporarily/permanently usable here? Are your existing upholstered pieces worth the investment of slipcovering or re-upholstery?

- Could you add floor-to-ceiling bookshelves or decorative-looking storage units in the hallway, foyer, or dining area?

- How much lighting will you need? Do you need track lighting for general illumination? Spotlights for your artwork? Uplights to create a romantic mood? Lamps for reading? Is it important that your living room be very brightly lit? (For more on lighting, see Chapter 8.)

- What is the best placement of furniture? We tend toward the obvious and assume a long wall is a good place for a sofa. But you can sometimes make a better use of space by placing the sofa at the end of the room or at an angle, or by using an alternative to a sofa. Furniture placement will be thoroughly covered in Chapter 4, but here you may want to consider whether the standard arrangement of a sofa and two chairs is actually best for your room. Perhaps two love seats might be better, or four club chairs around a large square coffee table.

- Would a mirrored wall be a good investment? Mirroring is expensive and certainly not advisable for every space. But if you have a great view, you might want to double its effectiveness by mirroring the opposite wall. Or you may be able to make the dining alcove seem larger by mirroring the back wall. (For more on mirrored walls, see Chapter 5.)

- Should you treat the living/dining area as one space or would it be better to divide it with a screen, bookshelf, or large tree? You'll want to think care-

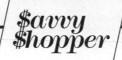
$avvy $hopper

UPHOLSTERING

For workmanship, you can expect to pay approximately $500 for reupholstering a sofa and approximately $350 for a chair. If you don't have an upholsterer, get estimates from department stores, which tend to be fairly reasonably priced. The advantage of dealing with a department store is that you don't pay the charge bill until the job is done correctly. It's harder to have this kind of leverage with an upholsterer.

Remember to add in the cost of your material. For a standard six-foot three-pillow sofa, you'll need about fourteen to sixteen yards. For a club chair, you'll need about eight yards. The exact amount will depend on furniture style, thickness of the pillows, and the size of the repeats in the fabric. The store or upholsterer will give you the exact measurements.

TIP
▽

"Buy at least one wonderful piece when you're furnishing. Each apartment is a period in your life, and you should have a souvenir from that period."
—Howard Kaplan

fully before you make this decision. The advantage to dividing the space is that you have two separate areas. The disadvantage is that each space is smaller, and may be cramped.

Sleeping Area/Bedroom

- Do you want the bedroom to be in the same style as the rest of the apartment, or would you like it to be dramatically different?

- Does the room or area lend itself to wallpaper? Although wallpaper is expensive, it gives a bedroom a finished look. Consider wallpapering two walls instead of all four—it's less expensive, but will still set the room off from the rest of the apartment. (For more on wall treatments, see Chapter 5.)

- Would you enjoy wall-to-wall carpeting in your bedroom? You can often find a carpet remnant large enough for a bedroom (For more on carpeting, see Chapter 6.)

- Have you shopped yet for sheets and other bedding? You may find that you can hit on a color scheme for the whole room by picking out the dominant color in a sheet or quilt pattern.

- Is the room large enough for a canopy bed or four-poster bed? This type of bed can be expensive, but it makes a big decorative statement, and is something that you'll take with you to every apartment.

- Is it necessary for you to have a traditional bed? If you have a studio apartment, it may bother you if guests can see your bed. In this case you might consider a Murphy bed or convertible sofa. Similarly, having a bed that folds up might allow you to use the bedroom as a den or office. But is the extra trouble of pulling out a bed worth the bother to you? Would this type of bed satisfy you psychologically?

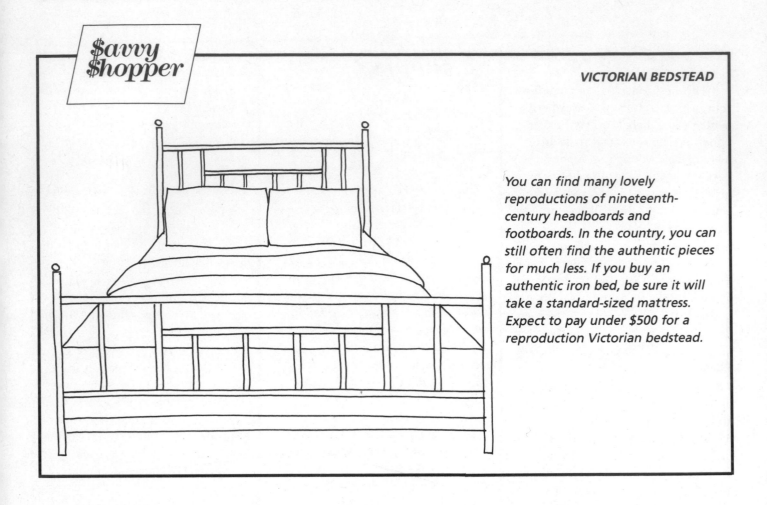

$avvy $hopper

VICTORIAN BEDSTEAD

You can find many lovely reproductions of nineteenth-century headboards and footboards. In the country, you can still often find the authentic pieces for much less. If you buy an authentic iron bed, be sure it will take a standard-sized mattress. Expect to pay under $500 for a reproduction Victorian bedstead.

 TIP

"A four-poster or canopy bed need not be confined to the bedroom. Use it in the middle of a studio apartment as a lounging area rather than investing in a convertible sofa that you might be buying as a compromise."
—*Richard Knapple*

 **$avvy $hopper**

CANOPY BED

There are many fine reproductions of canopy beds from every period. You should be able to find one for under $1,000. This is in rattan, but you might also find a well-made copy of an Early American or English style canopy bed in the same price range.

$avvy $hopper

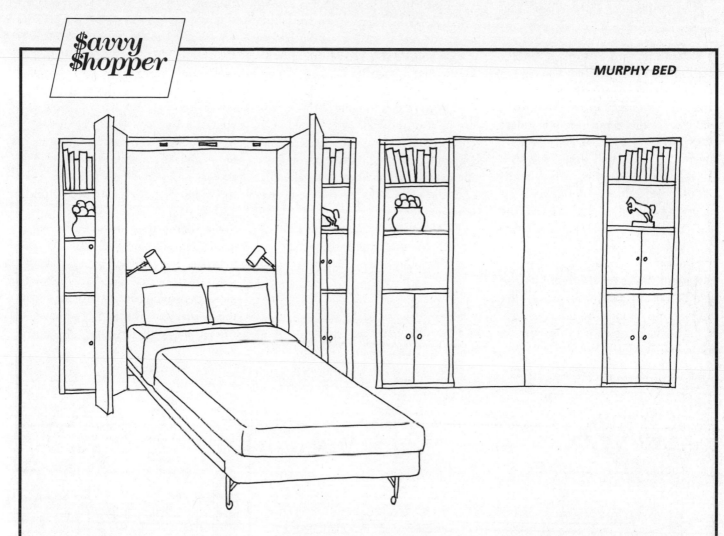

Murphy beds have been around for decades. They were out of style for years, but recently, they've come back into fashion in a major way. They are a wonderful alternative to a convertible sofa or having a bed in plain view in a studio apartment. A "Murphy bed" is, technically, the mechanism that allows the mattress to fold flat against the wall or be pulled down to bed level. However, when people refer to a "Murphy bed," they also usually mean the cabinet that closes the mattress off from view. With the renewed popularity of these beds has come an increase in the stylishness and, often, the expense—of the cabinets. You can now find cabinets in Formica, wood, mirror, or antique finish. Before you select a Murphy bed, it might be wise to look in the Yellow Pages and check out shops and showrooms that specialize in them.

Generally, the cost for the mechanism and frame, which is attached to the floor, is about $400. Cabinets will vary in cost, depending on the finish you select. For instance, a Formica laminated cabinet might cost from $600 to $800. Plain wood cabinets will cost less, while mirrored cabinets might cost double or triple that amount.

• Is your present mattress size large enough for you? Would you rather have a bigger mattress, or would it consume too much space? Mattresses and box springs come in four standard sizes: twin (39″ × 75″), full (54″ × 75″), queen (60″ × 80″) and king (78″ × 80″).

• Is your bedroom very small? Should you consider building a low platform for the mattress? A room with a carpeted floor and platform has a unified, uncluttered look.

• Do you need a place to store magazines and books by the bed? By one side or both? Could you use a table with a lamp on top? Would it be wiser to have small chests with drawers for additional storage?

• Do you need a good reading light by the bed or over it? On one side or both?

• Do you need to control the morning light in the bedroom? Would curtains or blinds close out enough light? Or would you prefer sheer curtains so the room is bright when you wake up? (For more on window treatment, see Chapter 7.)

• Is the bedroom noisy? Should you invest in interlined draperies for soundproofing?

Kitchen

• Do you have any pictures that could be hung in the kitchen? Most apartment kitchens are so small that even one picture can make a big decorating difference.

• Do you want to plant herbs at the windows, or put up hanging plants?

• Is there a wall that could be used for pegboard or a wire grid to hang spoons and potholders and towels, as well as other colorful kitchen accessories?

• Is there space to use as a bookshelf? Books are colorful in the kitchen.

• Is there space above the cabinets for storage? You can also use the top of the cabinets for vases of dried flowers, woven baskets, or other decorative items.

POWER STRIPS

WALL GRID

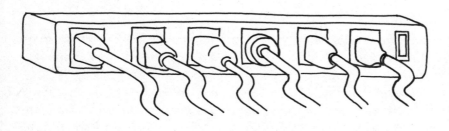

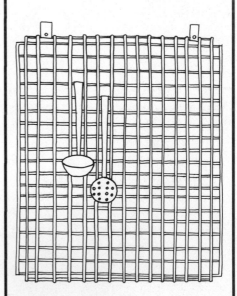

A strip of outlets called a "power strip" is much more convenient and attractive than having wires dangling from a dangerously overloaded wall outlet. A power strip across the kitchen counter, for example, will enable you to shorten the wires on your appliances so they can be plugged in neatly. Look for a power strip that has its own circuit-breaker and is electrically grounded for safety. Power strips are available for under $16.

Wall grid comes in sections that measure 18¾″ by 25″ and cost under $20. Perfect for closets or kitchens, the wall grid gives you easy-reach availability and makes storage space part of your design scheme.

• Does the window lend itself to a decorative treatment? Would curtains, shutters, or blinds give the room a lift? (See Chapter 7 for ideas.)

• Is the counter in good condition? Should it be covered or replaced with butcher block?

• Are the cabinets in good condition, or are they old, crusty, and in need of replacement? You might want to consider open or glassed-in shelves so that you can display your crockery.

• Is the flooring in good condition? Would a new floor treatment give the kitchen a real lift? (See Chapter 6 for information on floor tiles.)

• Do you have a broom closet in the kitchen that could be made even more useful if canned goods or cleaning solutions could be stored on the inside of the door? By using the broom closet to store cleaning materials, you may create additional space else where to store bulky pots and pans.

$avvy $hopper

PATTERNED CERAMIC TILES

Spectacular traditional and modern designs are available in Spanish, Mexican, and Portuguese glazed ceramic tiles for as little as $6 per foot. These tiles can be installed on the walls by a handy amateur. Consider ceramic tiles as a backsplash in the kitchen or as a beautiful table or counter top.

HOUSEWARES

FLATWARE. First shop for expensive flatware and get a feeling for the quality and the way the finer merchandise feels in the hand; then look for the best copy you can find. There's a wide range of very acceptable patterns and there's no need to spend a lot. You should be able to get eight place settings for under $50.

PLACEMATS. This is the place to splurge. For a few dollars you can find beautiful placemats that give the table a finished look. It's always worth a few dollars extra for things you look at every day. Plan to spend under $6 each.

COTTON NAPKINS. Any table is prettier when it is set with cotton or linen napkins, which cost $1.50 each.

WINE GLASSES. Although you can find many acceptable stemmed glasses for under $3, you might want the luxury of drinking orange juice from crystal goblets. Many beautiful crystal patterns can be found on sale for about $5 per glass.

CHINA. Beautifully designed china, pottery, or stoneware is available for less than $60 for a twenty-piece placesetting for four. You can often find specials on plates and cups so that you can put together your own set for four for about $25.

Bathroom

• Would you consider dressing up the bathroom with paint or wallpaper? It's small enough to be painted or wallpapered in a weekend, even by an amateur.

• Do you need new towels and accessories in pleasing colors?

• Do you want carpeting?

• How can you best utilize the back of the door—with a full-length mirror, or with wire shelves?

• Do you need a new shower curtain and liner?

• Is there room for a magazine rack?

• Do you need makeup lights?

TIP

"No matter what style you choose, shower curtains should always go from the ceiling to the floor. This can be done simply by moving the existing shower rod up to ceiling level. It creates the impression of a higher, more gracefully shaped room, and gives the shower curtain a finished, professional look."

—Lynn Levenberg

Closets

• Are your closets high enough to build in an extra shelf on top for storing luggage or out-of-season clothes?

• Can you put extra shelving on the backs of closet doors?

• Do you need the services of a closet specialist? This can be a pricey proposition because you're paying for an expert's time. But if you simply can't get all your possessions into the amount of space that you have, this could be a very worthwhile investment. An expert can sometimes almost double the space through very clever professional tricks. They also know about all the best equipment, the newest types of hangers, storage boxes, etc. Before hiring an expert, stop into a shop that specializes in closet supplies. It's possible they'll have an expert on staff who will help you make better use of your space at no cost because you'll be buying their equipment. (See also Chapter 9 for more on redesigning your closet.)

Decorating is like ballet: it looks easiest when it's done the best! Now that you've started thinking about all the aspects of design, from the aesthetic to the practical, I will introduce you to your decorators. These are top professionals who are famous for their great style and clever ideas. Before they start designing any apartment, they ask the questions you've just been asked. Now you'll see how they use the answers in creating wonderful rooms.

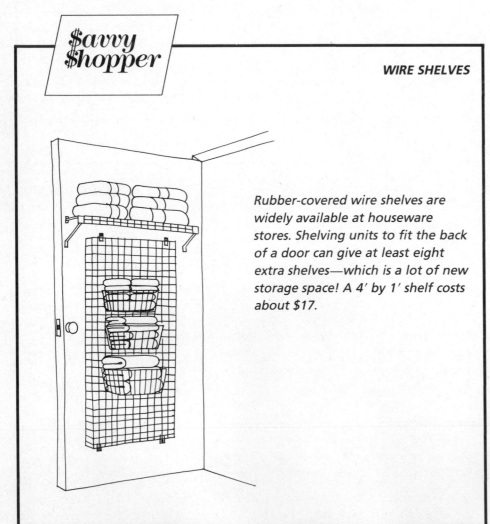

$avvy $hopper

WIRE SHELVES

Rubber-covered wire shelves are widely available at houseware stores. Shelving units to fit the back of a door can give at least eight extra shelves—which is a lot of new storage space! A 4' by 1' shelf costs about $17.

CHAPTER 2

MEET YOUR DECORATORS

Most of the beautiful places that you see in magazines were designed by decorators. There's a good reason for this: people who can afford the luxury of experienced advisors often work with professionals—and the result is the showplaces that you've seen.

Now you can have the same luxury. Along with picking up insider's tips and getting a wealth of ideas and knowledge, you'll also begin to see how each designer approaches a problem a little bit differently. Given the same space, one uses white, another black, and a third chooses a mélange of prints. Sometimes they follow rules, such as using small-scaled furniture in small rooms; sometimes they ignore the rules and use one enormous piece to provide an interesting focal point.

Here's a brief look at each of the decorators:

RONALD BRICKE is noted for his wizardry in using traditional furniture to create light, airy, and memorable rooms. He is particularly known for his attention to detail and handsome renovations which turn the most mundane rooms into unique spaces. In 1972, he opened his own firm (Ronald Bricke & Associates), designing residential and commercial spaces.

KIM FREEMAN has been a Decorating Editor for both *House Beautiful* and *Mademoiselle*. She is currently a freelance stylist with her credit line appearing regularly in such publications as the *New York Times*.

STANLEY HURA uses his dramatic and elegant decorating ideas in styling the J.P. Stevens model rooms, which are regularly seen in such magazines as *Ladies Home Journal*, *Cosmopolitan*, and *Woman's Day*.

HOWARD KAPLAN is one of the most knowledgeable figures in French Country furniture and decor. He designs furniture, pottery and lamps, and textiles and wallpaper for his French Country stores throughout the nation.

RICHARD KNAPPLE is famous for the model rooms that he plans for Bloomingdale's in New York, where he is Vice President of Interior Design. He travels regularly to Europe and the Far East in search of ideas and inspiration.

GERALD KUHN established his own company (Gerald Kuhn, Inc.) in 1979. Known primarily for architectural interior renovations, he specializes in residential and office design. He designs powerful spaces by using simple color schemes and layouts which serve as dramatic backgrounds for carefully chosen artwork and sculpture.

LYNN LEVENBERG is a former Decorating Editor of *American Home* and currently President of her own company (Lynn Levenberg Interiors, Inc.). She decorates residences and offices in New York, including the offices of *Cosmopolitan*. A long-standing devotee of English design, she employs the gracious colors, patterns, and furnishings of a London drawing room in even the most typical New York high-rise apartments.

TIM MEIER is Second Vice President of Design Construction/Branch Administration for Smith Barney. He is an architect as well as a designer, and his experience in designing offices across the country gives him a uniquely practical approach to decorating.

PAUL SHAFER and *JEAN WEINER* are partners in Cobuild, a New York design firm they founded in 1980. They specialize in space planning, treating every square inch of an apartment as if it were a jewel to be lovingly treasured and well used.

Although these designers are more likely to be planning chateaus or penthouses on Fifth Avenue than small spaces, they all relished the challenge of doing a knockout job on a budget. They are giving you the same tips they give their well-heeled clients, and they've even gone a step further: they've designed whole apartments using floorplans that are very typical of the cramped high-rise studio or one-bedroom apartment most of us have.

You'll meet your decorators in their own apartments on the next few pages, and you'll get a private glimpse of how professionals make their own personal choices. Their apartments are chock full of good ideas. As they explain their decision-making processes, you should be making notes and thinking about whether their approaches would be suitable for your place.

RONALD BRICKE

One basic rule in decorating is that small places call for less furniture and smaller pieces. "Scale it down and leave lots of air," the experts will tell you. But rules were made to be broken—as you can see from Ronald Bricke's living room.

In a relatively small (12′ × 20′) space, he has included an overscaled sofa, four huge lounge chairs, an enormous coffee table, two gargantuan vases, a pair of very big display cases, and a massive sculpture stand.

"This might have been too much furniture for a room twice the size," Bricke admits. But the room works because of color—or rather, the lack of it. Everything is white—walls, ceiling, sofa, lounge chairs and accessories. "White against white creates the illusion of openness," says Bricke, who used his decorating scheme as a problem-solving solution.

The sofa from a previous apartment was so large that it overwhelmed the room and an all-white scheme became a diversionary tactic. "Whenever you want furniture to seem smaller in scale, place it against a wall that is the same color. The edges aren't defined so the eye can't take visual measurements."

Bricke learned how tenuous illusionary space can be when he hung a painting. "The room suddenly seemed cramped because you realized how close the walls were to the furniture."

The painting is gone and the bare walls are the chalky white that one imagines in a Greek villa. This earthy texture was achieved by applying only a primer over the dirty white walls left

by the previous tenant. No top coat was used. The clean white brush strokes have created a sheer veil of color that gives the walls a soft whitewashed look.

Instead of decorating the walls, Bricke decorated the floors by staining and bleaching them. The parquet tiles were turned into a brown-and-white geometric pattern that adds vitality to the scheme. "If the floors had been the same color as the walls and the furniture, the room might have been bland. You need one strong element in a monochromatic color scheme. Sometimes it's in a painting or a rug; here it's the floor."

There are two seating areas in the living room—a sofa and two lounge chairs at the rear of the room, and two lounge chairs and a small carved wooden chair at the front. "In a rectangular room, having two seating areas enables you to take advantage of the space in front of the window and near the back wall. With a sofa in the middle of the long wall, these spaces often become dead areas."

The only non-white furniture—the display cases and sculpture stand—are of tinted green glass that reflects the whiteness almost in the way a mirror would. There is an uplight at the base of the sculpture stand which shines through the vase at the top, creating a pattern on the ceiling and supplying the mood lighting for the apartment.

"I've never used white for a client's apartment because most people are afraid of the upkeep of white slipcovers, white floors, and white walls. Yet the only way that you can make white—or any color—into a glamorous statement is by using it on almost every surface."

The small dining alcove is a charming continuation of the living room. A

Ronald Bricke's Apartment

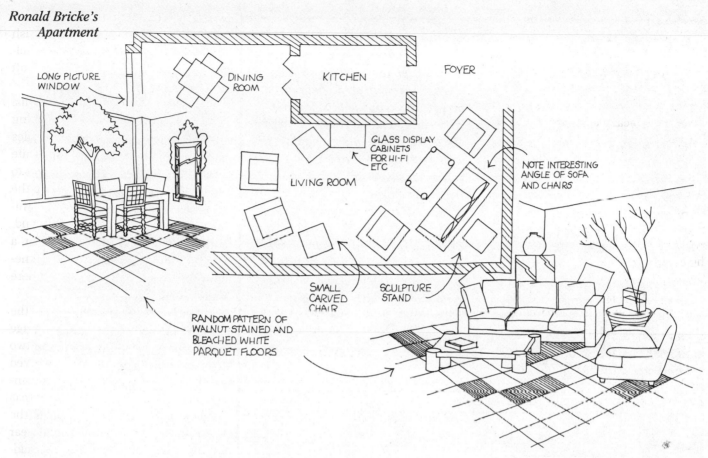

LONG PICTURE WINDOW

DINING ROOM

KITCHEN

FOYER

GLASS DISPLAY CABINETS FOR HI-FI ETC

LIVING ROOM

NOTE INTERESTING ANGLE OF SOFA AND CHAIRS

SMALL CARVED CHAIR

SCULPTURE STAND

RANDOM PATTERN OF WALNUT STAINED AND BLEACHED WHITE PARQUET FLOORS

white Formica table for four expands to seat six to eight. The chairs are ornately carved and provide a warm counterpoint to the white floors, walls, and table. A ficus tree adds color and is reflected in the Venetian mirror hung on the wall.

Bricke had planned to wallpaper the tiny kitchen in a large blue-and-white check, but when he couldn't find the right pattern he decided to paint the kitchen himself using a technique called "pouncing" (see box, page 20). The kitchen is a knockout. The bold blue-and-white check is cheerful and inviting, almost like having a country kitchen in the city. The freshness of the check makes it a perfect background for the baskets piled on the top of the cabinets and the copper cookware on the wall. Only a top decorator would realize that the reason the big

blue checks aren't overwhelming in this small space is because of the "pouncing."

Is This Style for You?

Bricke's living room is a wonderful choice if you want a very comfortable, very chic space. Its main drawback may be price. Even though you may find inexpensive copies of the seating pieces in Bricke's apartment, the fact that there are a number of them will drive your costs up. A lot of anything tends to be expensive.

The stylish effect of Bricke's living room is derived from using a dominant color scheme, in this case, white. Bricke's slipcovers are made of white stretch denim, a relatively inexpensive fabric. However, white slipcovers usually stay fresh only for about three

years. You can achieve a similar effect by applying the monochromatic principle with another color, such as beige, gray, or any pastel.

The brown-and-white geometric pattern floor treatment looks spectacular. This treatment is very expensive when it's done by professionals because the whole floor must first be stripped and then the squares for each color must be taped off and finished separately. In Bricke's apartment, a first coat of dark brown stain was applied and then allowed to dry before a second coat was added. The dark brown was then taped off so the white stain wouldn't run into it—and again, two coats of white were necessary. This isn't a complicated job, but it is time-consuming. If you have the time and patience to do it yourself, you'll have a custom job.

HOW TO... Use "Pouncing"

"Pouncing" enables you to use bold patterns and colors in a very understated way. This technique produces a subtly finished wall where a tiny bit of the background color shows through.

First, paint on your background color. (In his kitchen, Bricke used white.)

Then establish your horizontal and vertical lines. It is crucial that these be absolutely straight. You can't judge them by eye because the ceilings and floors in most buildings, particularly old ones, tend to slope. To establish your verticals, tack a string of the right length from the ceiling and weight it with scissors or some heavy object. Then rub chalk along the string and, holding the bottom of the string firmly, snap it against the wall. For the horizontal lines, use a carpenter's level (available at any hardware store).

Tape off the squares on the wall carefully, using either masking tape or thin transparent plastic from an art supply store. Instead of using a paintbrush, dab your second color onto the wall with wadded cheesecloth (this is the "pounce").

Immediately remove the tape so there isn't a buildup when the paint dries.

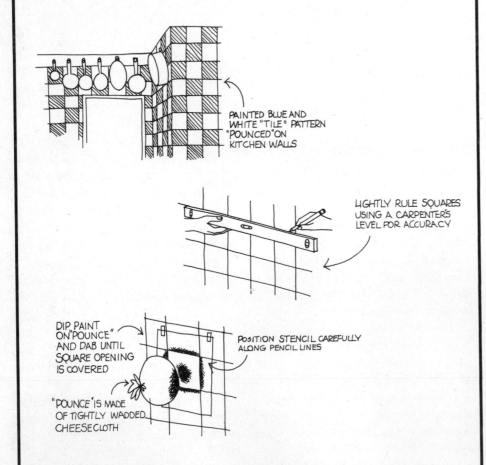

PAINTED BLUE AND WHITE "TILE" PATTERN "POUNCED" ON KITCHEN WALLS

LIGHTLY RULE SQUARES USING A CARPENTER'S LEVEL FOR ACCURACY

DIP PAINT ON "POUNCE" AND DAB UNTIL SQUARE OPENING IS COVERED

POSITION STENCIL CAREFULLY ALONG PENCIL LINES

"POUNCE" IS MADE OF TIGHTLY WADDED CHEESECLOTH

Kim Freeman

KIM FREEMAN

In New York, where "sleek," "chic," and "uncluttered" are decorating by-words, Kim Freeman chooses to go her own way. Her apartment is chock full of possessions, with collections of hats, tin boxes, Depression glass, old lace, antique perfume bottles, aging photographs, and art nouveau pitchers crowding each other cheerfully for wall and table space.

"Having one perfect object on a table isn't my style," she admits. "I like having all my possessions around me. It makes me happy to look at them. And I can always make room for one more piece."

Freeman's apartment is a small one-bedroom in a brownstone overlooking a park. The "kitchen" is a few old appliances pushed against the wall with some cabinets overhead. Rather than being hidden behind screens, the kitchen area is left open. The cabinets have been wallpapered and peek through a homemade built-in unit that holds glasses overhead and serves as a buffet and workspace.

"My way of decorating calls for having pretty things to show off," Freeman explains. Her passion is for old objects from almost any period. They needn't be expensive, unusual, or rare. But they must have the patina of age. "Old things have so much more warmth and interest than new things, which to me seem antiseptic and cold."

Freeman believes in starting a collection with one or two objects. "Live with them for a month or two and make sure that you love them and want more before you buy more," she advises. "A collection doesn't have to

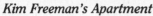
Kim Freeman's Apartment

SCALE, COLOR AND PERSONAL TASTE CAN UNIFY MANY UNRELATED OBJECTS

be totally by period or style. The person who is selecting the pieces gives a collection its unity. For instance, everything I buy is pretty and delicate and it all goes together because of the scale and color."

Many of Freeman's pieces have gained in value since she started collecting, but that is a happy coincidence. "Everyone always tells you to buy the best, but I think you should just buy what you love best."

Freeman bought most of her furniture at country auctions. Her favorite possession, though, is a white Victorian headboard with brass finials that was in the basement of an antique shop.

"Some of the best buys in antique shops are tucked away. Snoop around beneath and behind and ask a lot of questions," she advises. Kim isn't shy about bargaining with a dealer, but she doesn't expect any great reductions in price. "They've built in about

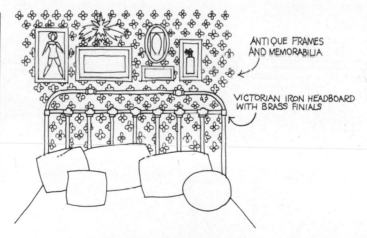

ANTIQUE FRAMES AND MEMORABILIA

VICTORIAN IRON HEADBOARD WITH BRASS FINIALS

10 percent leeway into the selling price. To get any more than that, you have to know the dealer very well or be very knowledgeable. You have to be able to say that you already have a collection with similar pieces and that you paid much less. Dealers respond to expertise."

In Kim's bedroom, two walls are papered in a tiny blue-and-white floral pattern. "By wallpapering two walls, you warm the room; by leaving the

other two walls bare, you cool it down so you feel less crowded."

Is This Style for You?

There are psychological pleasures as well as visual rewards from this very personal style of decorating. By using walls, shelves, and tabletops for possessions, you are surrounded by your own personal history. Each of the objects will remind you of a time and place. Thus, your apartment takes on a meaning that goes beyond decorating.

Decorating with collections and found objects can be less expensive than conventional decorating: you can cover an old sofa with a lovely patchwork quilt; you can repaint and stencil a secondhand table; you can add a handmade shade to an old lamp. Your investment is often more costly in time than money.

This form of decorating is an act of love and a continuing commitment. It can be done over time; indeed, that's the best way. Since every piece is a special "find," you can't expect to decorate your place from a department store in one Saturday.

For the room to remain lovely, you must have a sense of order, both in your displays and in your housekeeping. Collections that aren't cherished and well cared for tend to turn to clutter. If, however, the pleasure of being surrounded by your belongings is paramount, then decorating your apartment this way can turn into a lifetime hobby.

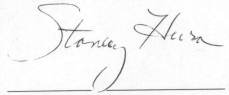

STANLEY HURA

If Stanley Hura had gone to a decorator, he might have done his apartment differently.

"I would never let a client start his place without thinking through everything he needs. I always tell my clients that nothing is more important than doing your homework. We discuss color and the way the apartment is being used, and I make extensive notes and floorplans. But for myself, I was like the shoemaker...."

After a busy day of designing, Hura likes informality, dressing in jeans and eating in the kitchen. Yet his place has the glossy elegance of a Cole Porter setting. On impulse, he opted for a palette of dark colors and theatrical drama. All of the walls of his two bedroom apartment are lacquered coal black, and reflect sensuously into sections of

bronzed mirrors. The ceilings are gold leafed and are as luxurious as the overscaled modular seating units upholstered in silk.

Visually, the apartment is a dramatic success. It's a wonderful place for parties and entertaining. Although the living room is only 14' × 27', it looks three times its size because of the mirrors.

Although Hura enjoys the glamorous effect of black walls, he still sometimes yearns for lighter colors and a more open feeling. Recently, he decided to have the best of both worlds, light and dark. The floors were stripped and refinished into off-white and the furniture slipcovered for summer in a beige-and-white linen. "Once you've established the backgrounds of an apartment, you can always adjust the overall look with slipcovers, lighting, or accessories," Hura says.

Asked about dark colors, Hura answers, "Black and very dark colors are a major commitment. These colors absorb light and they aren't great for daytime living unless you use mirrors, have light floors and create a very

Stanley Hura's Living Room

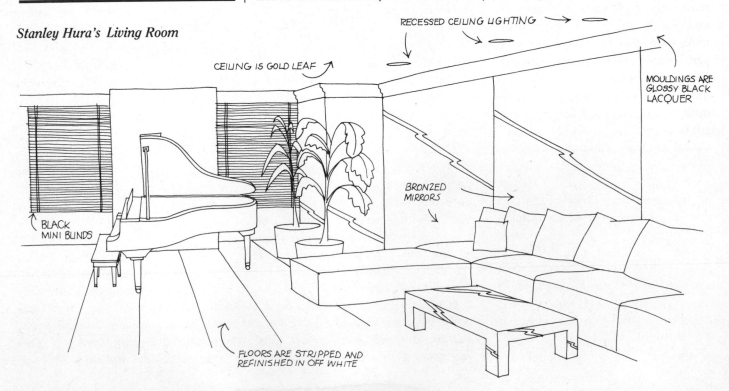

CEILING IS GOLD LEAF

RECESSED CEILING LIGHTING

MOULDINGS ARE GLOSSY BLACK LACQUER

BRONZED MIRRORS

BLACK MINI BLINDS

FLOORS ARE STRIPPED AND REFINISHED IN OFF WHITE

strong counterpoint of lightness with slipcovers or upholstery. But dark colors create a striking background for artwork and accessories. There is a certain glamour in colors like black and burgundy that can never be matched by pastels."

Is This Style for You?

If you want a glamorous apartment, then painting the walls black and using dark upholstery may be a wonderful choice. However, very dark colors, such as black, chocolate brown, and burgundy, need special handling. Hura started with brown-black and found the color wasn't strong enough to achieve the effect of pure black.

Hura's walls are lacquered—which is a very expensive process—but you can get a similar effect with a urethane-based paint. However, whenever you use a high glossy paint, you must be sure that the walls are in prime condition or the gloss will simply highlight the imperfections.

Mirrors are an integral part of the look of Hura's apartment. A wall of mirrors is an expensive investment and one that you might not want to make unless you own an apartment or plan to stay there for a very long while. Hura chose bronze mirrors because a tinted finish is more subtle than clear mirrors. (For more on mirroring walls, see Chapter 5.)

HOWARD KAPLAN

Howard Kaplan's apartment is more reminiscent of a French chateau than a New York loft. Kaplan converted a huge industrial space by stripping the ages-old plaster back to the brick and adding oak beams to the vaulted ceiling. This extraordinary space is the background for a priceless collection of French antiques and nineteenth-century paintings.

Kaplan's interest in French furniture started during a summer visit to France after college. He fell in love with the French countryside and bought a small thatch-roofed house. "For $1,500, you could buy a wonderful place then, but I only had $750 and so my place wasn't quite so wonderful." In fact, the roof had caved in by the time Kaplan returned.

Thatching the roof would have cost about twenty times the original price of the house. Kaplan solved that dilemma by having the entire house disassembled and brought back to New York in parts. He sold the house, piece by piece, along with the furniture. That paid for his next trip back to France and put him into the French antiques business.

"It's unlikely that anybody could afford this many beautiful pieces if they started collecting now," Kaplan admits. But he feels that one or two pieces of French Provincial go a long way. "These pieces are very strong elements in any room and elevate the style of the furniture around them."

In the kitchen area, the appliances are against the wall. Reproductions of the brass-rimmed pastry trays that one still sees in French bakeries hold a lovely ceramic collection. An ornately finished zinc bar creates a serving area.

Over the dining table, a chandelier with an opaline glass shade sheds a soft light. "A chandelier is like a piece of sculpture and should be beautiful even when it's not lit," says Kaplan.

The two large rooms are divided by a seventeenth-century Coromandel screen. In the bedroom, the focal point is an ornate reproduction eighteenth-*and* nineteenth-century style bed that Kaplan designed and sells for about $2,000. "I took the best of several styles and incorporated them," he explains.

Is This Style for You?

Unless you inherit a gold mine, it's unlikely that you could buy an impressive collection of nineteenth-century paintings and fine French antiques. However, when Kaplan began collecting, these pieces weren't as pricey as they are now. It is possible to buy very wisely, one piece at a time, and begin a collection that will grow in value.

Kaplan's advice when buying French country furniture is always to look for large pieces, such as a table or an armoire, because those pieces are very showy and will give the whole room a sense of style. He also advises that you comparison price the cost of reproductions with authentic pieces before making a purchase. "Quite often, a reproduction will be in the same price range as the real thing. And a new piece will never increase in value, while an older piece almost always will."

Although antiques appreciate, a better reason for buying them is that "you can develop a relationship with older pieces. They become a part of your life. We're surrounded by so much *ersatz* that it's wonderful to live with something of value."

Howard Kaplan's Apartment

17TH CENTURY KORAMANDEL SCREEN

OAK BEAMS FRAME VAULTED CEILING

RICHARD KNAPPLE

When you see a particularly handsome apartment, there's a good chance that what you *don't* see is every bit as interesting as the decor itself. That's the case with Richard Knapple's place. His one-bedroom apartment is small by any standard—a mere 550 square feet—and yet the space seems so open, uncluttered, and inviting that one can't imagine wanting even an inch more space. How does he do this?

The real secret starts with the behind-the-scenes planning. Knapple is vice president of design for Bloomingdale's and an avid collector of artwork and antiques. He travels constantly and needs to keep clothing for every season instantly available—he might be in China on Tuesday morning and Paris on Thursday evening. Add in his books, tapes, and business files, and Knapple's possessions could overwhelm a place twice the size. But Knapple avoided clutter because he planned the closets and storage space into the decor.

The largest closet in the apartment—a walk-in closet in the foyer—was redesigned to hold two tiers of hanging space. An extra wall was built inside to support additional shelves.

In the bedroom, Knapple refitted the closet to hold his stereo equipment and tapes, along with a top section for vases and sculpture. Every treasured square inch from floor to ceiling has been used. The bed is built on a low platform and the headboard opens from both sides. On one side, a file cabinet slides out; on the other, pillows and bedding are kept handy. Knapple debated whether to turn the platform into a storage area by raising it slightly, but decided against it because the bedroom is so small (a mere 11′ × 11′) that it seemed more important for the bed to be low, making the room seem more spacious.

The small linen closet was completely refitted with shelves that now serve as floor-to-ceiling drawer space.

*Richard Knapple's Closets
and Storage Spaces*

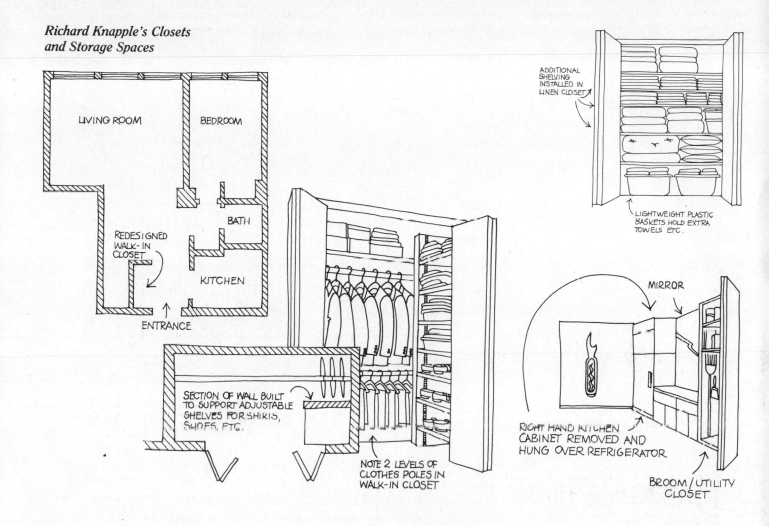

ADDITIONAL SHELVING INSTALLED IN LINEN CLOSET

LIGHTWEIGHT PLASTIC BASKETS HOLD EXTRA TOWELS ETC.

LIVING ROOM

BEDROOM

BATH

REDESIGNED WALK-IN CLOSET

KITCHEN

ENTRANCE

SECTION OF WALL BUILT TO SUPPORT ADJUSTABLE SHELVES FOR SHIRTS, SHOES, ETC.

NOTE 2 LEVELS OF CLOTHES POLES IN WALK-IN CLOSET

MIRROR

RIGHT HAND KITCHEN CABINET REMOVED AND HUNG OVER REFRIGERATOR

BROOM/UTILITY CLOSET

Knapple enjoys cooking and entertains often. His kitchen is galley-shaped, with the appliances on one side and a long counter with cabinets below on the other. Although there was an adequate amount of storage space for cooking utensils, there wasn't a pantry closet for brooms, the vacuum cleaner, etc. Knapple solved this problem by moving the end cabinet to the space over the refrigerator, which left enough room for a closet. The kitchen doors, which were almost never used, were reinstalled as "pantry" doors.

The kitchen is a very pleasant space to work in. Knapple covered the long linoleum counter with a slab of butcherblock and installed a wall-sized mirror over it to expand the space visually.

A giant can opener is a visual joke that adds a finishing touch to the space.

The guest closet holds bulky items, such as the folding chairs for the round black granite table in the hallway. Knapple reasoned that it's better to crowd the closet than the small entrance area!

Having cleared away the paraphernalia that might have cluttered the apartment, Knapple was able to decorate in the Japanese genre. At every point, less is more here. In the living room, a low platform runs the length of the room with futons on either end. Panels of bronzed mirror are on either side of the platform and make the space seem larger and more luxurious. The color scheme throughout the apartment—on the walls, ceiling, and

floor—is a rich shade of taupe. In the living room, the carpet covers the area between the mirrored panels. "It's more comfortable to lean against than a painted wall or mirror," Knapple explains.

Many of Knapple's decorating decisions were predicated on his lifestyle. He has a house in the country and rarely spends weekends in this apartment. Thus, he uses the apartment mostly in the evening and finds the dark color scheme a perfect nighttime setting. At the window, black metal vertical blinds add a polished look.

Lighting is an integral part of the design. Spots are focused selectively on the artwork, creating a soft, indirect light as well as calling attention to each individual piece.

Richard Knapple's Apartment

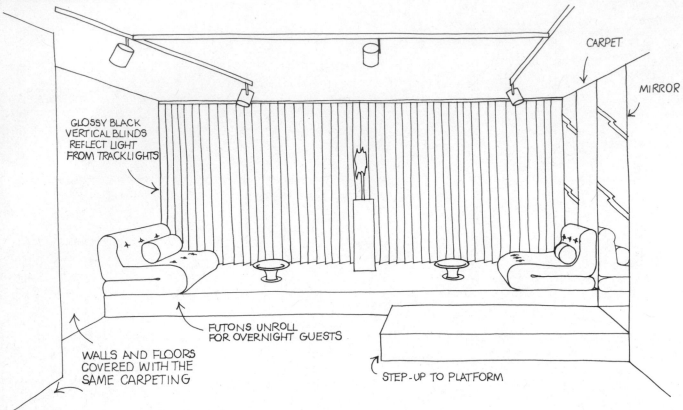

GLOSSY BLACK
VERTICAL BLINDS
REFLECT LIGHT
FROM TRACKLIGHTS

CARPET

MIRROR

FUTONS UNROLL
FOR OVERNIGHT GUESTS

WALLS AND FLOORS
COVERED WITH THE
SAME CARPETING

STEP-UP TO PLATFORM

Is This Style for You?

Knapple's approach is ideal for a small apartment. By decorating with low platforms, he creates an impression of higher walls and large, uninterrupted areas. This approach will always make a small space grander.

The deep taupe color scheme is ele-gant. It's restful during the day and glamorous at night. However, as Knapple points out, this color might be too dark unless the apartment were used predominantly in the evenings. Low platforms and a monochromatic color scheme could be used with a lighter shade very effectively.

It would be impossible to design an apartment this uncluttered without adequate storage for objects not being used. This may mean redesigning closets or editing possessions. The only objects that should be visible with this approach are those which you choose to show off.

GERALD KUHN

Having an office in your apartment is an invitation to disaster. One scenario includes papers strewn around, working materials visible, no place to entertain or escape from the "office." Gerald Kuhn's approach, however, is to use the "bedroom" as an office—which means the living room does double duty for sleeping and entertaining. This presents the classic dilemma of decorating around a bed. Rather than hiding the bed away, Kuhn made it the focal point of the living room. A gray carpeted platform across the front of the living room is the base for the mattress, which is wrapped in gray quilted cotton. This bold presentation turns the platform into a lounging area.

With the platform the focal point of the room, it became doubly necessary to mask the radiator (see box, page 28). Kuhn had a frame built around the window which became the support for the angled slats mounted wall-to-wall beneath a wide ledge that's used as a display shelf. At the side of the platform, an angled Formica cabinet provides a place for the television and magazines. The television slides out

*Gerald
Kuhn's
Apartment*

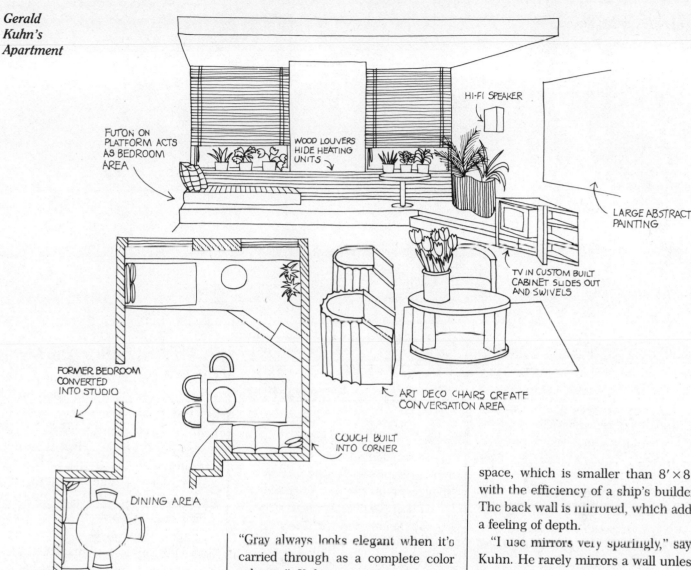

FUTON ON
PLATFORM ACTS
AS BEDROOM
AREA

WOOD LOUVERS
HIDE HEATING
UNITS

HI-FI SPEAKER

LARGE ABSTRACT
PAINTING

TV IN CUSTOM BUILT
CABINET SLIDES OUT
AND SWIVELS

FORMER BEDROOM
CONVERTED
INTO STUDIO

ART DECO CHAIRS CREATE
CONVERSATION AREA

COUCH BUILT
INTO CORNER

DINING AREA

and can be turned to any part of the room. When the cabinet is closed, it looks like a sculptural element rather than a practical necessity.

For years, Kuhn has collected art deco vases and furniture. Four gray velvet-upholstered chairs face a built-in leather sofa on the wall opposite the platform. The vases are in a lit glass cabinet and their brilliant finishes provide the only bright color in the room.

The apartment is painted gray, Kuhn's favorite color. It's a color that he discovered when he was decorating his first apartment, a small studio.

"Gray always looks elegant when it's carried through as a complete color scheme," Kuhn says. "It's the ideal background for artwork, it's easy to live with, and it gives a very serene feeling to a space."

In this apartment, Kuhn even painted the ceilings gray. He feels it's necessary to continue the wall color onto the ceiling in a new building such as his because the construction is usually so imperfect that a contrasting ceiling color only emphasizes the ragged workmanship. With the exception of the carpeted platform, the floors have been refinished in a pale sand color which gives the space its open feeling.

The dining area is in the hallway outside of the kitchen and directly in view of the front door. Kuhn uses this

space, which is smaller than 8′ × 8′, with the efficiency of a ship's builder. The back wall is mirrored, which adds a feeling of depth.

"I use mirrors very sparingly," says Kuhn. He rarely mirrors a wall unless the reflection is ideal, but decided in this instance that even though the kitchen could be glimpsed in the mirror, the feeling of additional space made the mirror a valid decorative element.

The focal point of the dining area is a beautifully designed pyramid-shaped shelf that holds a collection of baskets. The shelf was made by starting with a narrow base and building outward and upward, giving the shelf an interesting thickness and an unusual custom look.

A built-in seating unit across the back of the wall is covered with pillows covered in a gray silky-looking synthetic which can be removed for clean-

Gerald Kuhn's Dining Area

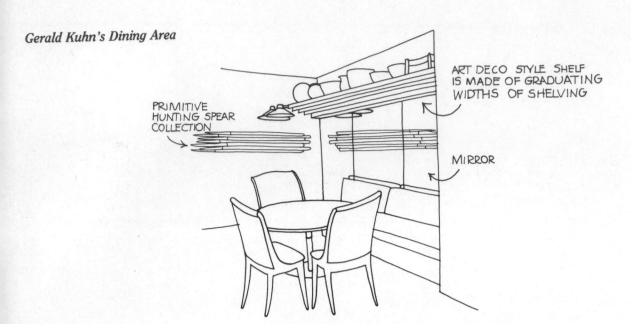

ART DECO STYLE SHELF
IS MADE OF GRADUATING
WIDTHS OF SHELVING

PRIMITIVE
HUNTING SPEAR
COLLECTION

MIRROR

ing. The two small chairs and round table are in proportion to the tiny space. Lighting is also kept in scale: a track with seven small cylinders, each with a 75-watt reflector bulb, creates a soft, even light and is much more attractive than bigger spots might have been.

"Most dimmers have a 600-watt capacity. You can divide that capacity any way you choose—but you can't exceed it because you risk an electrical overload. If you use 150-watt fixtures, then you can only use four spots. In a small space, four very powerful lights create a glare. You have to measure the effect you want with light along with the capacity of the dimmer."

HOW TO...
Cover a Radiator

A radiator cover is relatively easy to make and can become an integral part of your design. The four sides that make up the frame are of 2" × 4" lumber that can be cut to size at the lumberyard. The sides of the frame are attached to the wall. Slats are then added; they can be angled if you first nail triangular pieces of wood to the sides of the frame and then nail the slats to the triangles.

Is This Style for You?

If your office is an important part of your life, then Kuhn's approach would be ideal. It allows you to use the bedroom space efficiently without depriving yourself of an elegant living, sleeping, and dining space. The all-gray color scheme is calm and sophisticated.

The built-in platform can be a box structure or it can be a storage unit with a hinged top that lifts. The angled Formica storage unit was relatively expensive and built by a cabinetmaker for not much more than the cost of a good piece of furniture.

Lynn Levenberg

LYNN LEVENBERG

Most people take the easy way. For an apartment in a modern high-rise, they use the tried-and-true neutral color schemes, vertical blinds, and contemporary furnishings. Not Lynn Levenberg. In her L-shaped studio she opted for opulence, using a pattern-on-pattern approach that turned the standard shell into a cross between an English drawing room and a maharaja's summer tent.

Fabric and color are the key elements here. Blue-and-white-striped fabric-covered walls are the cheerful background to a sofa and armchair, upholstered in red embroidered antique Afghan fabric, yellow print undercurtains, and a canopy bed with nine separate patterns and colors, ranging from off-red to blue-green.

Lynn Levenberg's Apartment

NOTE WALL FABRIC IS REPEATED AROUND INDIAN AND AFGHAN PRINTS

BLUE AND WHITE STRIPED FABRIC ON WALLS

HEAVY AFGHAN RED EMBROIDERED FABRIC

TURKISH RUG

OVERSIZED PATTERNED THROW PILLOWS

CANOPY BED IS SURROUNDED BY NINE PATTERNS AND COLORS

BEDROOM AREA IS SEPARATED BY RUFFLED DRAPERIES

PROFUSION OF BOLD PATTERNED PILLOWS ADDS A DRAMATIC TOUCH

HOW TO...
Make a Canopy

To hang the ruffled valance, install curtain rods on the ceiling in a square slightly larger than the bed. Then gather the fabric onto a hemming tape. When you insert the drapery prongs into the pockets in the tape, it automatically pleats the fabric. For the side panels, hang shorter curtain rods to the correct length and follow the same procedure for gathering the draperies. (For how to make a crown canopy, see page 53.)

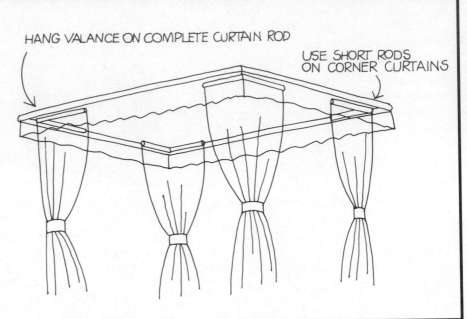

HANG VALANCE ON COMPLETE CURTAIN ROD

USE SHORT RODS ON CORNER CURTAINS

Even with the addition of Turkish rugs on the floors and oversized patterned throw pillows, the effect is surprisingly harmonious.

"There's an immediate feeling of warmth in entering a room that has patterned walls and upholstery. It's welcoming in a way that no modern room can possibly be," Levenberg says.

Although the pleasures of being in a richly patterned room are obvious, many shy away from this approach because it looks expensive and it seems too difficult to coordinate the fabrics. "In truth, a modern decor with a neutral color scheme can be more expensive to complete," says Levenberg. "With very simple furnishings and wall treatments, you need outstanding accessories and art. In a patterned room, you don't notice the accessories—you feel the room and its surroundings. No individual piece stands out."

In other words, the whole is more important than the parts. To achieve this, Levenberg has developed a formula for mixing patterns:

"You have two choices if you want a patterned room. The first is to do the whole room in one pattern—walls, upholstery, and curtains. This can be very effective. The other choice is to use at least six different patterns. The biggest mistake you can make in working with patterns is to use too few."

Okay. So one is fine, two is boring, four is better, and six is ideal. How do you find six patterns that work together?

"The key is to keep varying the scale. For example, use a large-scale (25″ to 30″ repeat) floral print for the sofa and draperies; a texture or plaid on the easy chair; a medium-scale print (16″ to 20″ repeat) on pull-up chairs; and small-scale prints (3″ to 4″ repeat) on pillows and lamp shades. You can measure the repeat yourself. Keep a list. No two fabrics should be in exactly the same scale—they will fight each other. In different sizes, they will complement each other.

"Arrange the fabrics on the floor and step away from them. Squint with your eyes almost closed. If all the fabrics run together with no one pattern jumping out at you, that's a good indication that the colors blend well.

"Sometimes it's effective to inject a brilliant splash of color into the room for added drama. This might be in the form of an ottoman or round hassock which is covered in solid, jewel-toned satin or taffeta. Anything solid will stand out in a room filled with prints. This means if you use one solid, it must be very important."

The finishing touch in Levenberg's apartment is the canopy bed that serves as a secondary seating area. It's partially curtained off with draperies, which separates the space without dividing the room. "I decided on this approach rather than hiding the bed away," she explains.

Although the wealth of Indian and Afghan prints gives the bed an exotic cast, it's actually a very clever use of curtain rods (see box above).

Is This Style for You?

Creating a patterned environment is truly an act of love. It calls for attention to detail and numerous decisions—how to cover the walls, the lamp shades, the sofa, chairs, and pillows. Some of these decisions can be made less time-consuming by working with a pattern that has coordinates. These are widely available, but tend to be more expensive than finding fabrics individually and putting them together yourself.

The main drawback to creating a patterned room is that it implies permanence. You are selecting wall and window coverings that are made to measure and might not fit into your next place. If, however, you are planning to be in your apartment for an extended period of time, this is an ideal way of creating a very rich looking, comfortable home.

Working with fabrics is either the most expensive or the least costly way of decorating. If you are willing to do a lot of work yourself, then a patterned room can be the greatest bargain in decorating. For the price of the material, you can have fabric-covered walls, interesting window treatments, beautiful pillows, and unusual lamp shades. If you have to pay others to do the labor, then it becomes prohibitively expensive.

Lynn Levenberg did much of the work herself. She stapled the blue-and-white fabric to the wall and made the bed curtains herself. The fabric-covered mirror would have been expensive in a shop, but Levenberg covered a frame with cotton batting and stapled a scrap of fabric around it. Similarly, the lamp shades and pillows—all important finishing touches—are easy to make. To complete this look, whether you're using pastel florals or Eastern designs, use lots of pillows in different sizes and fabrics.

R. Timothy Meier

TIM MEIER

Tim Meier's apartment has grown up with him. When he was an architectural student, the apartment was makeshift, with a drafting board that dropped from the wall. After graduating, he got rid of the drafting table, painted the walls a dark blue, and bought an Oriental carpet. Now Meier says his apartment is still in transition.

"It's almost impossible for anyone in the design field to say their apartment is perfect. Something that may have been right two years ago doesn't seem right with two years more experience. We change and our tastes change and there's no reason to think this won't be reflected in our furnishings."

Meier is preparing his apartment for its next period. He's now buying fine furniture as a long-term investment and hopes that changes in the future will be more subtle. The only pieces that will stay are the Victorian claw table and the bentwood chairs. These pieces were relatively inexpensive but are classics that will mix with any style. He has recently been upgrading the backgrounds—walls and floors—to give a suitable home to the expensive leather Chesterfield sofa he has ordered.

Three of the walls are upholstered in a lightly textured beige wool, which was chosen for its neutral quality as background for the artwork that is yet to come. The light color of the fabric also emphasizes the woodwork around the windows—one of the great assets of many townhouse apartments—and serves as a sophisticated counterpoint to the recently stripped brick fireplace wall.

Fabric-covered walls are a luxurious touch in any apartment, but here there was also a practical reason: the walls were badly damaged by a fire, and it would have been almost as costly to refinish them as to cover them with fabric. The beige floor carpeting is an almost exact match for the wall coverings.

"Light colors make a place seem larger. I like the opulence of dark shades, but they are difficult to live with and make a room seem smaller."

Meier chose the lighting before selecting his furniture. "You can sit on pillows and be comfortable if the mood is right—and that's what lighting does." Four can lights on the ceiling give enough illumination for the room. Although Meier considers three feet from the wall the ideal placement for track lights, his track is in the middle of the ceiling so that both sides can be lit by the same source.

The spotlight directed toward the fireplace wall shows off one of Meier's favorite possessions, the original archway from the building where he lives. He's collected this type of "urban archaeology" for years and believes that banisters, fireplace mantels, and ornamentation from old buildings are still a good buy.

"Fine pieces are getting more scarce," he admits. "But you can sometimes strike a deal with a contractor at a demolition site if you have some cash in your pocket and the means to cart away your find immediately."

Is This Style For You?

When Meier was younger, he bought inexpensive pieces that were in good taste and suited his budget. "At some point, though, you begin to realize that you should begin investing in furni-

Tim Meier's Apartment

"URBAN ARCHAEOLOGY" WALL DECORATION IS FROM THE BUILDINGS ORIGINAL DOORWAY

47

ANTIQUE VICTORIAN CLAW-LEG DINING TABLE WITH CONTEMPORARY BENTWOOD CHAIRS

ture and backgrounds that you want to live with over time rather than continuing to buy replacement pieces."

Meier's starting point for long-term decorating was the backgrounds. The wall covering and the carpeting are of the finest quality, meant to be enjoyed for years. He delayed buying a new sofa until he could afford the best quality leather Chesterfield.

This approach takes patience. It means living with old furniture until you can afford pieces that are long-term investments. However, if you start with the backgrounds, as Meier did, even inexpensive furniture will benefit from well-considered surroundings.

PAUL SHAFER AND JEAN WEINER

Since Grecian times, columns and porticos have been the signature of classically elegant decorating. Yet you don't need temple-sized rooms to make use of these decorating tools. Quite the reverse: you can start with an ordinary-sized space and make it seem much grander by using columns to create the feeling of splendor. That's what Paul Shafer and Jean Weiner did in the living room of Shafer's one bedroom apartment.

Shafer wanted to break away visual-ly from the bowling alley–shaped 12′ × 20′ living room without making any major architectural changes.

"Two of the most effective ways to create the impression of more space are by using lighting and by changing the sightlines," says Shafer. He attacked the sightlines first. These are the lines of vision that you see from each space in the apartment—when you enter the apartment, when you are

Paul Shafer's Apartment

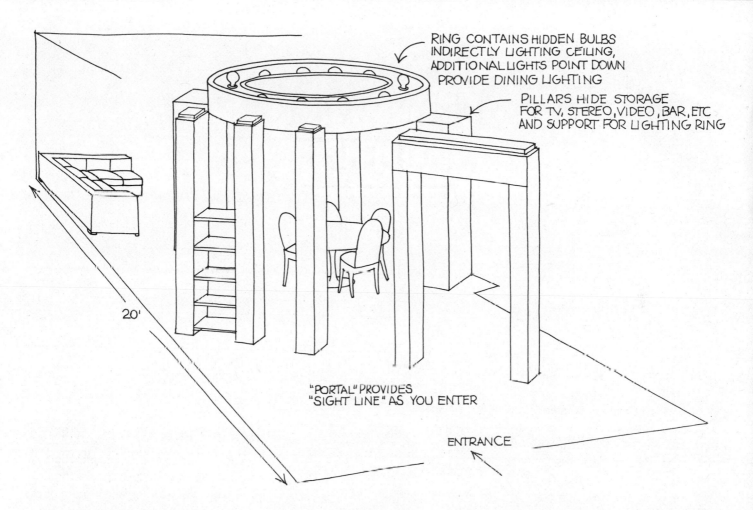

RING CONTAINS HIDDEN BULBS
INDIRECTLY LIGHTING CEILING,
ADDITIONAL LIGHTS POINT DOWN
PROVIDE DINING LIGHTING

PILLARS HIDE STORAGE
FOR TV, STEREO, VIDEO, BAR, ETC
AND SUPPORT FOR LIGHTING RING

20'

"PORTAL" PROVIDES
"SIGHT LINE" AS YOU ENTER

ENTRANCE

seated, or when you are standing in a particular part of the space.

In this apartment, the hallway and living room were completely visible from the front door. There were no surprises. Shafer changed that. A "portico"—two columns with an overhead lightbox—creates a theatrical entranceway as well as blocking the sightline from the front door into the living room.

Now you are guided into the living room at an angle. "It's up to you to decide what you want people to see and when you want them to see it," says Jean Weiner. From the portico, one walks into a rotunda of light and columns—at exactly the spot where it will be most appreciated.

A large round overhead fixture defines the space as surely as a wall would. "By lighting one area more brightly than the next area, you call attention to the space and separate it visually," says Shafer. The effect of the lighting is reinforced by the columns surrounding it.

Although the "portico" and the "rotunda" appear as decorative elements, they are totally practical. "In a small apartment, you don't have the luxury of doing something just because it's visually pleasing," says Shafer.

In the entranceway, the pillars support the overhead light box. In the living room, all of the pillars have storage drawers, and of course the columns support the lighting at the top. It's no

accident that none of the columns touch the walls. By pulling furniture into the middle of the room, the boundaries of the walls aren't defined and you have a feeling of greater space.

Is This Style for You?

A rather ordinary apartment has been turned into an extraordinary space with the use of columns and the light ring on the ceiling. The pillars and light rings were custom designed and made to order for this space. Shafer is thinking long-term. If he were to move, it's unlikely that he'd be able to use these pieces in the same way in his next apartment.

CHAPTER 3

PLAN YOUR BUDGET

It's time to take the next step: planning what to buy. Here you'll have to be very tough with yourself. You'll need to work out a budget that reflects your personal and financial priorities—and that you can stick to! With the step-by-step guide in this chapter, you'll be able to plan a budget that lets you decorate with style.

HOW MUCH CAN YOU AFFORD?

The first step in assembling your decorating budget is to determine how much money you can spend when. Be honest with yourself as you fill in the following preliminary chart. It won't do any good to pretend that you'll somehow have more money for decorating than you really will.

1. I have $_____ $ _____
   available to spend
   now
2. Optional: I am $ _____
   willing, in addi-
   tion, to charge
   $_____ on my
   credit card.
3. I plan to set aside $ _____
   $_____ for
   decorating during
   the first year.
4. I plan to set aside $ _____
   $_____ for
   decorating during
   the second year.

TOTAL
DECORATING
BUDGET $ _____

As you can see, this budget has a provision for decorating in stages. More on that later in the chapter.

WHAT'S YOUR SCHEDULE?

The second major consideration in planning your budget is deciding how quickly you want to finish the job. Do you want to decorate all at once, or are you willing to do a little at a time over several months, even years? The advantage to decorating quickly is that your apartment will be comfortable almost immediately. "I'll buy better pieces for my next place. But meanwhile, I want to come home to a nicely furnished apartment," said a recently divorced man who is quite satisfied with his decision to decorate all at once.

But the flip side here is that you might not be able to buy the best of everything if you're decorating quickly. Remember, too, that if you try to do too much too fast, you may be constantly short of money, which isn't fun. If your urge is to decorate all at once, you want to be sure that you won't feel deprived passing up an expensive dinner with friends in order by buy a lamp. Your other needs are as important as any furniture that you buy—and your budget will only be successful if it takes all your needs into account.

CONSIDER THE FUTURE

As I mentioned in Chapter 1, it's important to be realistic about how long you plan to stay in your apartment. If you expect to be there for more than two years, then a portion of your initial budget should probably be spent on the ambience of the apartment—what the decorators call "backgrounds." How much you'll need to allot will depend in large part on the condition of walls and floors and how elaborate you want the window treatments to be. If you plan to be in your apartment for only a year or so, however, it would probably be wiser to invest in portable pieces that you can take with you—freestanding bookshelves rather than built-ins, for instance.

Even though you may love your present apartment, you'd need a crystal ball to know what the future holds. You may be transferred, decide that you'd like to live in another part of town, have your building go co-op, have a love affair with a person whose apartment is larger than yours. Our lives are open-ended, and the way we furnish our apartments should reflect this flexibility.

SETTING PRIORITIES

"The starting point of a decorating budget," says Ronald Bricke, "should include everything a person really wants—a game table, a wonderful sofa, a brass bed, a beautiful desk. Obviously, one can't have everything, but people can have more than they suspect. Before you start cutting corners, choose the one or two things that you really consider important and see if you can't have them."

Just as there are no longer proper skirt lengths or universal dress codes, so there is no preordained type of furnishings necessary for an apartment to be considered complete. There's nothing that says you need a dining table or even a bed; a futon may serve you as well. Every individual has his or her own set of priorities. For example, when Howard Kaplan moved into his first apartment, he ignored the cracking plaster and sagging floorboards of his Greenwich Village walk-up and spent his limited budget on a handsome French country armoire and a sleigh bed that could be used as a sofa during the day. "I never put money into backgrounds," Kaplan says. "If your furniture is beautiful, then people won't notice the walls."

On the other hand, Tim Meier's priorities were track lighting and luxurious beige wool wall coverings with matching carpeting. To Meier, furniture is secondary.

What is on your must-have list? A romantic four-poster bed? A wonderful stereo system? Would you sacrifice a dining table so you could have a down-filled reading chair? Or is your dream a platform bed and wall-to-wall carpeting?

Keep in mind that no room has to be filled with knockout furniture. But every room should have a few interesting pieces—an antique or secondhand chair that is a conversation piece, art that is worthy of notice, a rug that adds color and warmth, an expensive glass bowl as the centerpiece for the dining table or coffee table. These are the things that will be remembered and will give your rooms style. They'll also help the transition period if you opt for long-term decorating.

If you want antiques and investment pieces that you can keep with you always, you should also think up front about the sacrifices you may have to make in terms of comfort. Perhaps you're like the young literary agent who slept on a mattress on the floor for a year while she paid off a fine painting that has since increased many times in value.

Use the chart on the next page to make a preliminary list of your decorating priorities and to assess their costs. Fill in the list in pencil. As you go through this book and get more ideas, you may want to change your priorities.

How do your totals match your budget estimate on page 34? If your costs are way too high, can you go down the list of top-priority items here and move some to second or even third priorities? Should you wait to invest in that antique hutch until you have your sheets and towels? Are you sure you want to invest in the window treatments you have chosen if you plan to move in three years? If you juggle the figures, you will probably find that you can come up with a satisfactory solution to the budget dilemma. Chances are it will involve the very practical method of decorating a bit at a time.

DECORATING IN STAGES

Since few of us can afford the luxury of buying everything we want at once, it makes sense to decorate in carefully planned stages. While there are no set rules—we each have our own priorities—the following guidelines (beginning on page 42) may give you a starting point for your planning.

In filling out this chart, use actual prices. Now is the time you should be shopping and thinking and shopping some more; you should be making notes and getting estimates. The more you know about the costs of decorating, the easier it will be to accommodate your needs in your budget.

If you plan to decorate in stages, rank your expenditures by priority. When the chart is complete you will have your totals for each stage of your decorating plan.

Decorating Budget

	ESTIMATED COST	TOP PRIORITY	SECOND PRIORITY	THIRD PRIORITY
LIVING ROOM				
Sofa	$ _____	$ _____	$ _____	$ _____
Coffee Table	_____	_____	_____	_____
End Tables	_____	_____	_____	_____
Lounging Chairs	_____	_____	_____	_____
Bookshelf	_____	_____	_____	_____
Storage Unit	_____	_____	_____	_____
Lamps	_____	_____	_____	_____
Track Lighting	_____	_____	_____	_____
Rug/Carpeting	_____	_____	_____	_____
Pictures/Artwork	_____	_____	_____	_____
Window Treatment	_____	_____	_____	_____
Desk	_____	_____	_____	_____
Painting	_____	_____	_____	_____
Refinishing Floor	_____	_____	_____	_____
Tree/Plants	_____	_____	_____	_____
DINING AREA				
Dining Table	_____	_____	_____	_____
Dining Chairs	_____	_____	_____	_____
Lighting Fixture	_____	_____	_____	_____
Buffet/Storage/Bar	_____	_____	_____	_____
BEDROOM				
Mattress/Box Springs	_____	_____	_____	_____
Headboard/Harvard Frame	_____	_____	_____	_____

Side Tables   _____   _____   _____   _____

Lamps   _____   _____   _____   _____

Chest of Drawers   _____   _____   _____   _____

Dressing Table   _____   _____   _____   _____

Dressing Table

Mirror   _____   _____   _____   _____

Rug/Carpet   _____   _____   _____   _____

Painting/Wallpaper   _____   _____   _____   _____

Window Treatment

KITCHEN

Cabinets   _____   _____   _____   _____

Cooking Utensils   _____   _____   _____   _____

Plates/Serving Pieces   _____   _____   _____   _____

Lighting   _____   _____   _____   _____

Pictures/Decorating   _____   _____   _____   _____

Painting/Wallpaper   _____   _____   _____   _____

New Countertop

Flatware/Glasses   _____   _____   _____   _____

BATHROOM

Shower Curtain   _____   _____   _____

Towels   _____   _____   _____   _____

Bathmat/Carpeting   _____   _____   _____   _____

Extra Shelves/Storage   _____   _____   _____   _____

Mirror   _____   _____   _____   _____

Lighting   _____   _____   _____   _____

Paint/Wallpaper   _____   _____   _____

FOYER

Table/Console   _____   _____   _____   _____

Lighting Fixture   _____   _____   _____   _____

Picture   _____   _____   _____   _____

Rug   _____   _____   _____   _____

Painting/Wallpaper   _____   _____   _____   _____

TOTAL

$ _____ $ _____ $ _____ $ _____

DECORATING DILEMMA

"I'm Not into Grandeur."

"I sometimes think I was born into the wrong century," says Amelia Stern, a twenty-three-year-old art director. "All of my friends are very ambitious—they want to get ahead in their jobs and have expensively furnished apartments. That's not what I care about. I want to be free. When I've saved enough money, I'd like to travel until I'm broke and I need another job. I'm happiest without too much responsibility."

Amelia was lucky enough to find a rent-controlled studio apartment with lots of light and now she wants to furnish it tastefully—for a minimum amount of money.

"I don't have an emotional attachment to furniture," she told her designer. "I wouldn't want to polish antiques, even if I could afford them. I just need a place to eat and sleep and some simple seating for a date or friends. I'm not into grandeur, but I do want the place to be tasteful and interesting-looking. Put quite simply, I want to own some furniture, but I don't want the furniture to own me."

DESIGNER: KIM FREEMAN

Amelia is an eccentric. She can afford to be casual about her job because she is so talented that everyone who sees her portfolio wants to hire her.

We furnished Amelia's place in two Saturdays. The first Saturday we spent shopping for a storage bed that would be her major piece of furniture. We chose a white Formica platform bed that has drawers underneath. On the same day we bought rush matting and tossed it on the floor wall-to-wall.

The next Saturday, we went wild in the sheet department. We bought zebra-striped sheets and pillowcases, and a leopard-printed quilt. The patterns are strong and they look great with the floor mats. We were lucky

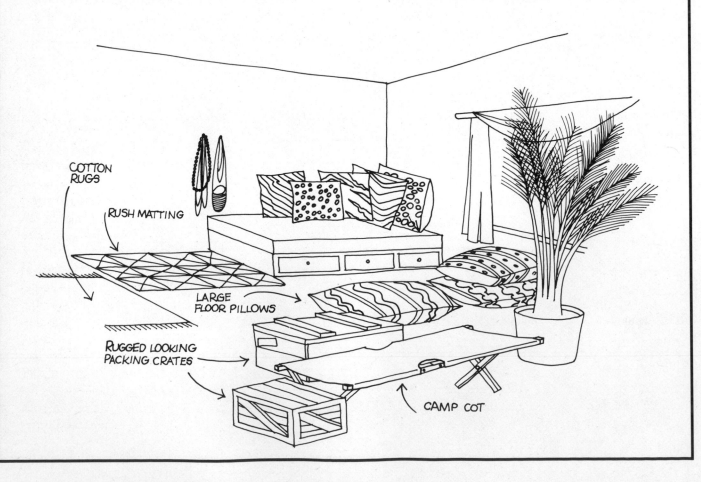

COTTON RUGS

RUSH MATTING

LARGE FLOOR PILLOWS

RUGGED LOOKING PACKING CRATES

CAMP COT

DECORATING DILEMMA

enough to find zebra-striped china and coffee mugs that match the sheets.

Amelia doesn't care about furniture and she's equally disdainful of convention. She didn't want standard curtains. "They're so boring. Let's do something that's fun." We got a bamboo pole from a nursery (about $2) and put it up from the ceiling with cup hooks. Tossing a length of fabric over the pole has an offhand campsite chic.

Amelia personalized the apartment by hanging her collection of African beads and straw bags as a wall montage. We found some packing crates on the street to use as tables. She bought three big pillows for the floor, and her decorating was done. Even though we spent very little, the animal prints give the apartment a lot of style. In fact, Amelia likes the apartment so much that she just accepted a promotion. "I'm not in any rush to leave here," she says. "Maybe I'm getting house proud!"

DECORATING DILEMMA

No Money, but Rich, Rich Taste

Suzannah Cantrell didn't always live in a one-bedroom apartment. Until her recent divorce, she lived with her husband in one of the legendary plantations outside New Orleans. All she took from the marriage was her heirloom silver and her fabulous rich-girl taste. She knows that draperies should always be interlined, that her best color is Wedgwood blue, and that her bedroom should inspire male fantasies. Having grown up with beautiful things, she knew how to duplicate the look.

Suzannah was shocked when she realized her New York friends rarely invited their dates to dinner. "Why, darlin', you're missing the opportunity of a lifetime," she tells them. Suzannah's first concern was finding the right place for her dining table. "It has to be very comfortable," she told her decorator. "I don't like skimpy little tables. You should always have enough space to put everything out so you don't have to keep jumping up. After all, I won't have any help to serve," she says with a tinge of regret.

The living room should be "just plain pretty," she said, adding, "I want an apartment where people drop in for a drink and stay for the evening."

Suzannah is now an assistant editor for one of the fine small publishing houses. She often brings manuscripts home in the evening and needs a desk and a place for papers.

When she's alone, Suzannah's favorite place is her bed. "My dream is a romantic bed—something plantation style. Lots of pillows, lots of frills, and very feminine."

DECORATOR: LYNN LEVENBERG

Suzannah has a great sense of personal style and she intuitively knows how to dress and decorate so she'll look her best in the colors around her. She is a willowy blonde who accents her southernness with picture hats and long, lace-edged dresses in watercolor pastels. We designed her apartment in the same fragile color palette as her clothing.

The foyer and living room are painted Wedgwood blue with white molding. The floors had been stained dark by a previous tenant and we had them polished and waxed to a high sheen. We used the foyer as a dining area, since it is large enough for an L-shaped banquette. The base of the banquette is plywood; the top was hinged so it can be opened and the base can be used for storage. The plywood was painted the same wedgwood blue as the walls. It becomes super-comfortable with the seating and back pillows, which match the peach/

DECORATING DILEMMA

blue/white/celadon–patterned tablecloth. The table is a skeleton table from a display store—there's no reason to spend a lot on a table nobody will see.

Suzannah grew up with fine blue-and-white china. Her mother had collected it for years. Suzannah loves the look and eventually she'll bring a few good pieces from home. Meanwhile, though, she knows that blue-and-white china is always stylish, and that it usually takes a connoisseur to tell the difference between inexpensive copies and the real thing. We built a shelf over

the banquette to hold a collection of modestly priced pieces.

To give Suzannah the luscious-looking living room she wanted on a budget, we bought inexpensive furniture and covered it with beautiful fabrics. The peach/blue/celadon/white floral theme in the hallway is continued in the living room, giving a unity to the area. The sofa has a large-scale pattern (36″ repeat) as a counterpoint to the cotton chintz pattern on the pillowed armchairs (3″ repeat). The floral draperies are a 25″ repeat

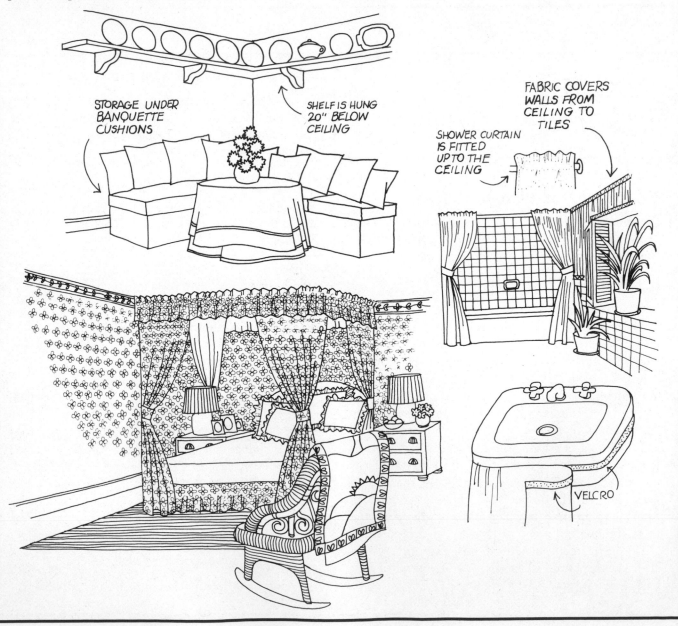

DECORATING DILEMMA

pattern, and the pillows range in between, so the effect is lots of pattern—and yet the patterns blend into one another because the repeats are different in scale.

The key to making inexpensive furniture or draperies look expensive is the finishing. All the furniture is piped in peach cord and the draperies are ribbon edged. Suzannah is very talented with a sewing machine and she made her own slipcovers and draperies. She claims the slipcovers were easy—that she pinned the fabric inside out and basted it before sewing it on the machine.

Books and storage were a concern. The bookshelves were from a store that sells unpainted furniture. We edged them with carved molding from the lumberyard and painted the whole unit a high gloss Wedgwood blue to match the walls. To cover the convector against the back wall and give Suzannah more storage space, we built bookshelves straight across. This gives the window wall a very finished look.

The bedroom is the prettiest room in the apartment, and is totally feminine. We used the same color scheme in the bedroom, but made celadon, rather than blue, the

dominant color. It's important to have a unified scheme in a small apartment, but if you're using prints you can slip into a second color so the rooms blend together without being exactly alike.

Suzannah splurged on a wallpaper and draperies that coordinate with the fabrics in her canopy bed. A border around the ceiling gives a finishing touch. The curtained bed treatment was a 4″ repeat striped floral pattern lined with a narrow pin stripe companion geometric pattern. A pastel rag rug in yellow, peach, white, and celadon completes the picture.

Fabrics and finishing touches like the welting, ruffles, ribbons, and lace trims on the pillows give the apartment a very expensive look. We used fabric because Suzannah was willing to shop for days and days to find good buys. We could have had a very similar look for half the price if we had used sheets.

We continued the romantic look into the bathroom. The walls above the tile were shirred with fabric, and Suzannah made shower curtains in another print that matched a skirt for the sink.

$avvy $hopper

MATTRESS AND BOX SPRINGS

Box springs and mattresses are available in a wide range of prices; many believe you should buy the very best you can afford and keep them for many years. However, as practical as that seems in theory, it might not necessarily be advisable. In one apartment, a double bed may be appropriate; in another, a queen-sized bed may be more desirable. If you're not sure what your future plans are, then don't splurge on a top-of-the-line mattress!

You should be able to obtain a double-bed-size mattress and box springs for under $350.

GLASS TABLE TOP

Even the plainest stainless steel table base will become a handsome dining table if it's covered with a ¾″ glass top. Thick glass is almost synonymous with elegance. In addition to width, you can also specify color. Green, gray, or bronze tints are particularly smart-looking. Department stores and furniture shops often have standard sizes at reasonable prices; custom glass tops are ordered through a glazier. When shopping, request prices for rounded corners and bevelled edges. Clear plate glass that is ¾″ thick sells for about $25 per square foot; ½″ glass is about 40 percent cheaper. Bronze glass is about 20 percent more expensive.

Stage 1

Absolute necessities: sofa, box spring and mattress (or other sleeping arrangements), lamps, painting the walls. The best buy in decorating may well be a can of paint. There is no bigger immediate visual change than painting the walls a lovely color or refreshing them with a clean coat of paint. Unless your floors are in awful condition, ignore them in your first stage of decorating.

Ronald Bricke's advice is to "spend the first part of your budget on the upholstered pieces. They should be the best that you can afford. On a limited budget, don't start with the 'secondary' furniture—the end tables, little cabinets, decorative accessories. The table that is supporting a lamp doesn't have to be wonderful, but the furniture you are sitting on should be!"

Stage 2

More necessities: dining table and chairs, side chairs in the living room, perhaps one rug. A sisal rug (see Chapter 6) or an inexpensive rag rug in front of the sofa will suffice until you've finished making your major purchases. Beautiful window treatments are a lovely addition to any room, but usually come under the heading "finishing touch"—something that you'll attend to when you've bought your most important pieces.

Stage 3

The luxuries. This is the most enjoyable part of decorating. Now you are finishing the apartment with a handsome coffee table, side tables, perhaps an antique for character, paintings and accessories.

Remember, there are as many variations on these stages as there are people decorating apartments. While most of us would consider a sofa a Stage 1

$avvy $hopper

NINETEENTH-CENTURY FRENCH COUNTRY ARMOIRE

At $3,000, this is likely to take a large bite out of anybody's budget, but it's also a great investment. In French country furniture, the two best buys are the armoires and the farm tables. "Many of the older pieces aren't as expensive as the reproductions," says Howard Kaplan.

necessity, some might feel that a beautiful rug or painting is an absolute priority.

TIPS ON BUYING MAJOR PIECES

An expensive piece of furniture is a long-term commitment. A good decorating plan for your first apartment will include a few important pieces that you will enjoy now, as well as later.

Ronald Bricke suggests that you keep the following tips in mind when you purchase your major pieces:

• No piece should be exaggerated in size—too large, too bulky, too deep, too high, or too long.

• The sofa should be a standard length. Six feet is a wonderful size because it fits into almost any apartment layout. It will also fit into almost any elevator when you're moving.

• Always consider ceiling height when you buy a bookshelf, armoire, or étagère. Even if your present apartment has a ten-foot ceiling, there's a very good chance that a future apartment will have an eight-foot ceiling.

• Invest in a 6' × 9' size rug. It's a size that will always work because it fits in front of the sofa and allows enough width for a chair on either side. (See Chapter 6.)

When you're debating between an authentic piece and a reproduction in the French country style, keep in mind the following advice from Howard Kaplan:

• If it's big, buy the real thing. The big pieces were originally made by the peasants for their own farmhouses, whereas the smaller and more delicate pieces were made for the chateaus. There were always more poor people—and thus there are still more of the big, showy armoires and farmhouse tables around and their prices are relatively lower than the smaller pieces.

• If it's a copy, buy the plainest style. Lots of carving tends to look fake.

• Shop for the real thing before you buy a copy. This will give you a feeling for the woods. In French country furniture, there's a wide price differential between pieces with similar styling. You should know what the best looks like so that you can better judge the quality of a reproduction.

• Avoid French country styles with a painted wood grain. This is a style that was popular a few years ago and it's an indicator of a second-rate piece.

DECORATING DILEMMA

Start from Scratch—and Decorate Your Way!

When Carol Willis divorced her husband, Arthur, she was twenty-eight and had been married for five years. "Our marriage never really worked," she recalls. "Even his taste in decorating was different than mine. He liked leather sofas and modern art. I like pastels and romantic-looking furniture."

Carol loves to read and Arthur loved entertaining. "This time, I want to enjoy my apartment as much when I'm alone as when I have company," she told her designer. "I can live with a dining table that doubles as a desk, and I don't care if the bed shows. I just want everything to be pretty, and for the apartment to have a very finished look."

Carol let Arthur keep their old apartment and furnishings in exchange for $10,000. This became her budget for decorating her new studio apartment. "It is the first place I saw. It's not perfect. There's not enough light and there's not even a dressing room. But the rent is right and I love the neighborhood."

The only serious problem with the apartment was the walls. Although the building is only twenty years old, it had apparently "settled" badly and the resulting hairline cracks on the walls would be expensive to refinish.

"This is the first time I've decorated an apartment for myself. Before I married Arthur, I lived with two other women and we were all more interested in husband hunting than in fixing up our place. This time around, I want my apartment to be a real home."

DESIGNER: STANLEY HURA

Carol was starting from scratch and she needed to buy everything—sheets, towels, and kitchen supplies—along with the furniture and accessories for her studio. In order to come in under budget, we decided to use sheets for the fabrics.

The sheet pattern we chose gave us our color scheme. It was a J.P. Stevens check with lavender, peach, cela-

don, and white—very subtle colors that were easy to work with. I chose the lavender for the walls and matched it to lavender wall-to-wall carpeting. Even the ceiling was painted lavender.

It's important to have a unified background for a small apartment. By matching the walls, ceiling, and floor, a space seems larger and more serene. Then you bring out the color with accessories, slipcovers, and artwork. Your background sparks everything around it. The white track on the ceiling and the white Formica dining table/desk look very pristine against the lavender.

Carol didn't want to spend a lot of money fixing up the cracked walls. We avoided this expense by using a very light "sand" paint that gave a texture to the walls and filled in the cracks.

Carol expects to move into a larger apartment within the next few years and she wanted furniture that would go with any style she chooses for her next place. Wicker was an ideal choice for her. It's delicate enough for her present studio and it blends in well with almost any contemporary or traditional furniture style.

Carol didn't want a convertible sofa for her bed. "It's too much trouble to make up in the morning," she said. Instead, we used a double bed with enough throw pillows to make it comfortable for lounging. The bedspread was made from sheets, and the pillow covers on the bed and chairs were made from coordinates of that pattern. An inexpensive celadon green rag rug defines the lounging area and separates it from the reading and desk areas.

The building across the street blocks the light and necessitated a window covering that would ensure privacy. White vertical blinds let the sunlight in while still blocking the view. We put pillows on the convector to give Carol a window seat—which is both a romantic touch and a way of tying the color scheme together.

Stage I

Carol wanted to decorate in two stages. Although she could afford to buy everything at once, she wanted to go slowly to make sure that each of her purchases worked before she went onto the next stage.

DECORATING DILEMMA

In Stage I, the apartment was painted, the carpeting and vertical blinds for the window were purchased, along with the bed, dining table, and chairs. During this period, Carol pulled the dining chairs over to the sofa when she had company.

Wicker furniture is available in all price ranges. The better wicker is relatively expensive, but it can be worth the price because it's sturdier and will last longer. Carol opted for top-of-the-line because she planned to keep each piece for years.

Carol's other major Stage I expense was track lighting. She wanted the whole apartment softly lit. This meant installing a rectangular track so the lights could be directed to all parts of the room to eliminate glare.

Carol's luxury during this period was in buying beautiful towels, pretty sheets, and kitchenware. "I don't cook much, but I'd like stylish plates, nice stainless, and a few cotton napkins. I'm at the point in life where everything I touch should be pleasing."

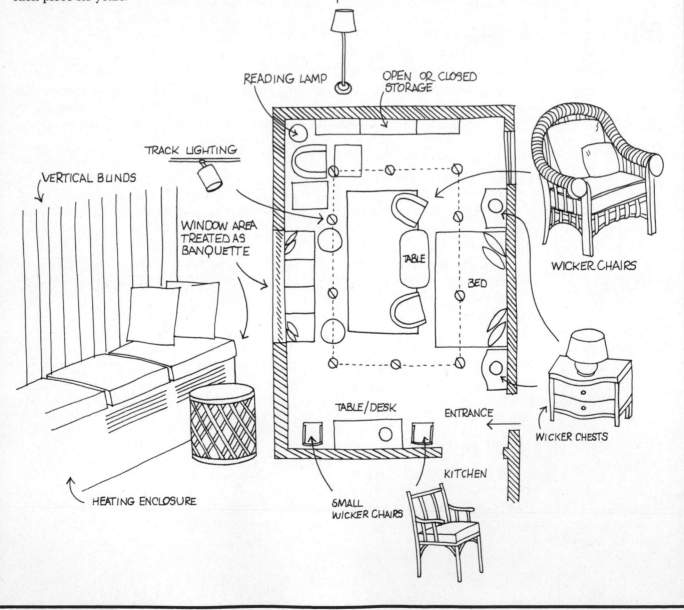

READING LAMP

OPEN OR CLOSED STORAGE

TRACK LIGHTING

VERTICAL BLINDS

WINDOW AREA TREATED AS BANQUETTE

WICKER CHAIRS

TABLE

BED

HEATING ENCLOSURE

TABLE/DESK

ENTRANCE

WICKER CHESTS

KITCHEN

SMALL WICKER CHAIRS

DECORATING DILEMMA

Bed	$400
Formica desk/dining table	180
Two dining chairs	200
Painting	400
Track lighting w/ten fixtures, track and electrician, dimmer	900
Carpeting w/installation	750
Sheets/towels	225
Kitchen utensils/toaster oven, wastebaskets, housewares, etc.	500
Plates/serving pieces/stainless and glasses	350
	$3,905

Stage II

Carol was very comfortable with her purchases. The monochromatic background made the apartment seem immediately homey, so she went straight into the second round of decorating and bought the rest of the furniture, the pillows, bookcases, and standing lamp, and chose her fabrics.

Carol used a coordinating sheet and quilt pattern for all of the upholstery. A quilt was fitted to the box springs and another was fitted to the mattress to give the bed an upholstered look.

Carol was fortunate in having a good local seamstress.

This is an important consideration when deciding whether to have furniture and pillows custom covered. If you don't have an inexpensive seamstress or upholsterer, it might be less costly to buy ready-made pillows and bed coverings.

Two wicker chests	$1200
Three table lamps	180
Reading Chair	350
Ottoman	150
Side Table	150
Reading Lamp	45
Three bookshelves/ storage units	1200
Vertical blinds	400
Two wicker easy chairs	600
Coffee table	250
Rug	125
Sheets/quilts for upholstery and pillows	200
Pillows	180
Workmanship	200
Two drum tables	120
Plants/vases/artwork/accessories/ baskets	500
	$5,850
Total Cost of Decorating	$9,755

MIXING STYLES

When shopping for new furniture to mix in with the furniture you already own, keep in mind that it's

• Easy: when most of your furniture has very straight lines and you are adding an ornamental antique. Very straight lines are good with curved or softer lines (for example, a Parsons table with a bentwood chair).

• Harder: when your background style and the style you are mixing in both have very straight lines. For example: contemporary furniture is difficult to mix with the linear, boxy mission style.

• Hardest: mixing two styles that both have curved lines, such as a French cabriole leg table and an art nouveau chair.

GETTING THE BEST BUYS

Here are some practical pointers to help you get the most for your money, and stay within your budget.

• When you're pricing furniture, be sure to get the total price—which includes taxes, delivery charges, and any extra cost for pillows or trims.

DECORATING DILEMMA

Paying in Stages—by Credit Card

When Melissa Evans took her first apartment, she decided to offset the costs by furnishing it so that it could be shared with a friend until she could finish decorating. Melissa planned to decorate in stages, using her credit card to its limit. After each group of purchases, she paid off her debts and started again. Melissa's apartment is a small L-shaped studio, and she told her decorator that she wanted the design to be chic, shareable, and inexpensive.

DESIGNER: GERALD KUHN

"The major challenge in Melissa's place was to give her two separate beds, plus places to eat, work, and sit, all without crowding—in a space that measured less than 400 square feet."

Kuhn started with two platform beds built end to end. Each platform top is hinged to create a storage box. The floor and platforms were carpeted to give the appearance of built-ins. During the day the platforms form a long, elegant sofa, covered with brightly colored pillows and fitted comforters.

The room appears spacious because of the placement of furniture. The back wall, usually a wasted area, is the starting point for the platforms, which end at a long desk/dining table which juts out from the wall. Under the table is a file drawer that can't be seen from the sofa.

The rest of the space is as open and uncrowded as an apartment three times its size. The window wall, originally a clutter of convectors and air-conditioning units, is now covered by twenty feet of vertical blinds. The verticals are reflected into a mirrored wall in the alcove, which seems to double their length visually.

Color is an important part of the decorating plan. Kuhn used gray throughout—in the carpet, the vertical blinds, on the walls and ceiling. "The smaller your space, the more important it is to simplify your color scheme," he points out. The bright touches here are in the pillows and the books on the shelves over the platforms. The high shelf gives more than twenty feet of storage space without cluttering the walls.

Stage I

In the first stage, we painted, built in the platform beds, bought the mattresses, the table, two of the dining chairs, and the halogen lamp that is used for overall illumination in the apartment. The bookshelf was also added at this time. Usually bookshelves are not a Stage I priority, but Melissa was able to get a better price from the carpenter by having the shelves built at the same time the beds were constructed.

The lumber for the bookshelves was much more expensive than the lumber for the beds. This is because the bookshelves are made of high grade lumber, but the platforms—which were to be covered with carpeting—are made of less expensive lumber. The top grade of lumber will be smooth; lesser grades are rougher and will be knotted. The top grade is about four times as expensive as the lowest grade, so it is important to select the right wood for the job.

Painting	$400
Carpentry/platforms	350
Lumber/platforms	110
Carpentry/bookshelf	150
Lumber/bookshelf	110
Two single mattresses	250
Table	140
Two dining chairs	100
Halogen lamp	125
Total	$1,735

Stage II

In Stage II we carpeted the apartment and installed twenty feet of vertical blinds. Melissa bought the last two dining chairs, the desk lamp (which doubles as a

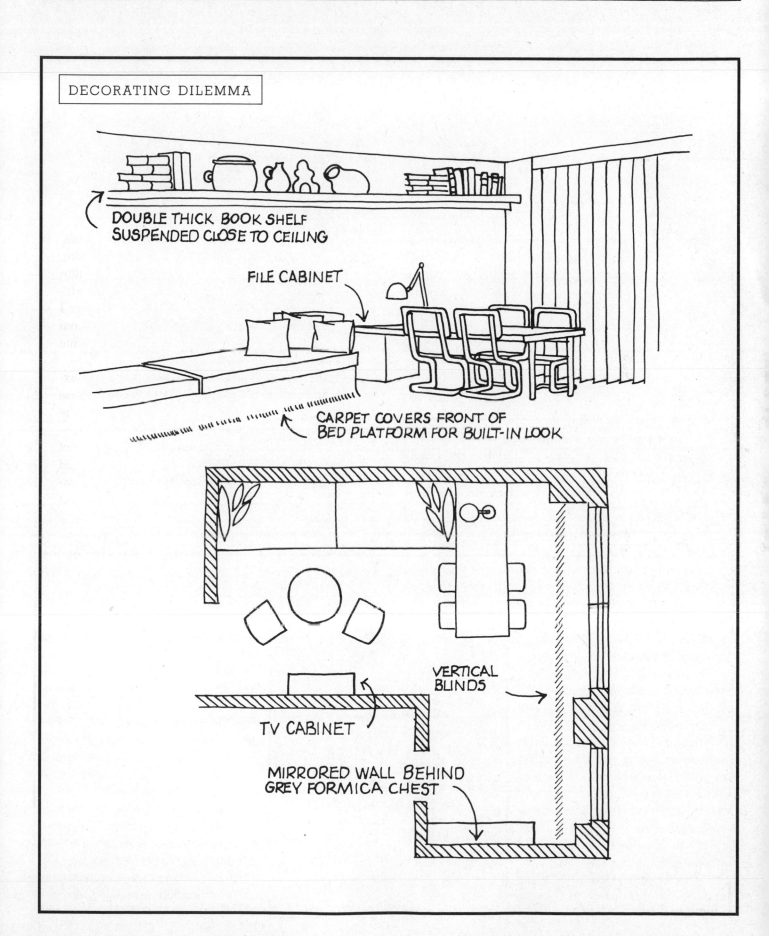

DECORATING DILEMMA

DOUBLE THICK BOOK SHELF SUSPENDED CLOSE TO CEILING

FILE CABINET

CARPET COVERS FRONT OF BED PLATFORM FOR BUILT-IN LOOK

VERTICAL BLINDS

TV CABINET

MIRRORED WALL BEHIND GREY FORMICA CHEST

DECORATING DILEMMA

reading lamp for the bed), and the file cabinet. She also bought the gray Formica chest for the alcove.

Carpeting	$525
Vertical blinds	350
Dining chairs	100
File cabinet	60
Desk lamp	35
Formica chest	500
	———
Total	$1,570

Stage III

Mirroring the back wall of the alcove was a luxury, but the mirroring adds sparkle and light to the space and is well worth the cost. In this period Melissa also bought two black canvas "butterfly" chairs for the living room and a chest for the television, as well as new linens, pillows, and the covers for the bed.

Mirroring	$500
Two canvas chairs	130
Chest	300
Sheets	150
Matching comforters	150
Throw pillows	150
	———
Total	$1,380

Stage IV

At this point, Melissa was ready to splurge on the finishing touches: a deep red drum-shaped plastic coffee table and a big tree that adds a touch of color to the back wall.

Coffee table	$350
Tree	125
	———
	$475
Total cost of decorating	$5,160

These "extras" can be real budget busters.

• Always ask whether you can buy a floor sample. Furniture lines change every six months, and retailers have to sell the old floor models to make room for their new lines.

• When you're buying in a small furniture shop, ask for a discount for cash. You should be able to get 5 to 10 percent off the purchase price.

• Whenever possible, buy upholstery in the standard fabrics. These tend to be much less expensive than the alternates.

• There are almost always sales in August and January in home furnishings.

TIP

"Rattan has great style and mixes beautifully with furniture of any period. In seating pieces, your choice of upholstery fabric will give the piece its casual or sophisticated look. With white canvas, for instance, it will be crisp and modern; with batiks or silk, it will be very elegant."
—*Richard Knapple*

• Decorators buy from special showrooms. There's usually a building in every city where the showrooms are for "the trade only." This means that you need a decorator's card to buy. This furniture is generally more expensive and more highly styled than department store furniture—but decorators get a discount of about 40 percent. If you know a decorator, ask if you can split the discount.

• Warning: Beware of the trendy. Rule of thumb: The more expensive the item is, the more conservative you should be in choice of color and design. Save your trendy purchases for disposables, such as posters, inexpensive accessories, pillows.

PARSONS TABLE

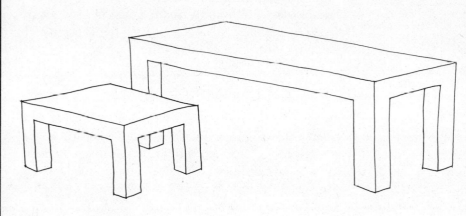

Parsons tables were popularized in the twenties by the Parsons School of Design, where they were adapted from the understated lines of a real parson's table. They have remained an important contemporary piece ever since because they adapt so well to so many uses, depending on their size: as a dining table, desk, end table, coffee table, etc. A Parsons table is particularly interesting when used as a foil for antiques or character pieces.

You can obtain a Parsons table for about $120. Unpainted furniture stores can order them for you in any dimensions you'd like at affordable prices.

BENTWOOD CHAIRS

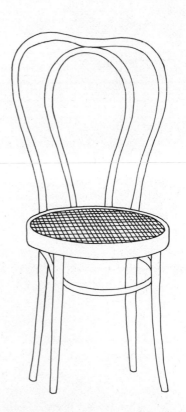

Bentwood chairs have long been a classic. They mix particularly well with modern, "hardedged" styles such as the Parsons table. Reproduction Bentwood chairs can be had for under $50.

WINGBACK CHAIR

Wingback chairs are often on sale through department stores, and are one of the best buys in traditional furnishings. By doing some careful shopping, you can find a fine-looking, well-upholstered style for under $300.

DECORATING DILEMMA

Shopping with a Discerning Eye

Bella Winters has always had two ambitions: to live in New York and to be a travel agent. "I know it's crazy. While all my friends were dreaming of becoming famous writers or corporate executives, my ambition was to start my own agency." Three days after arriving in New York from Des Moines, she landed her first job, as a secretary for a medium-sized agency, and two days after that she found her first apartment. It's a walk-up in a so-so neighborhood with adequate space, big windows, and lots of light. "Next to the Taj Mahal, this will always be my favorite place," she vows.

Bella couldn't afford to spend much money on the apartment, but she wanted it to be special—something with character. She also needed good work space, for she knows that she will have to bring work home from the office for the first few years. In addition to closet and drawer space for her own clothing, she needs enough space for her files. "But," she warned her decorator, "I don't want the place to look like an office."

DESIGNER: KIM FREEMAN

We gave Bella a very romantic, old-fashioned look even though we used very few old pieces. The apartment is too small to be crowded with lots of furniture. And we knew in advance that we'd have to make storage room and include a desk or table that Bella could use when she brings work home.

We solved the storage problem and the question of a headboard very neatly by putting a file cabinet at the

CEILING MOULDINGS AND BASEBOARDS PAINTED DIFFERENT COLOR THAN WALLS

LENGTH OF LACE DRAPED OVER DOWEL

FILE CABINET UNDER SCARF ACTS AS HEADBOARD

REPRODUCTION EARLY AMERICAN ÉTAGÈRE

CHINESE URN IS COFFEE TABLE BASE

PARSONS TABLE PAINTED 2 COLORS

DECORATING DILEMMA

end of the bed. It has enough height to serve as a back for pillows. We got the file cabinet from a used office supply store—always a good place to find file cabinets, chairs, and desks. The cabinet we bought wasn't beautiful, but you'd need X-ray vision to know that: we covered the top with a scarf and put out Bella's jewelry in little straw baskets. We found a very handsome Chinese urn at a flea market, which became a ideal coffee table with a small round glass top.

The only expensive piece in the room is an étagère. It's a reproduction Early American piece that cost about $1,500 and it's quite handsome. Along with giving Bella a considerable amount of extra storage space, it is an impressive piece of furniture. Whenever you're furnish-

ing inexpensively, it's always best to try to get one outstanding piece of furniture.

Bella has a very discerning eye. She loves lace and she's very careful about the details that give an apartment character. We found some lovely old linen pillow shams at a secondhand shop in the neighborhood. Bella edged them in lace and tossed the pillows on the tailored gray-and-white plaid bed coverings.

The finishing touch in the apartment is the length of lace that is casually tossed over a rod at the windows. It looks romantic without being traditional and gives Bella's apartment the extra measure of charm that makes a place memorable.

• Sheets are one of the best buys in fabrics. They are available in coordinating colors and patterns and are affordable. It's wise to buy at one time all of the sheets you'll be needing, since the patterns change every six months.

• Workmanship is one of the highest costs in decorating. Any work that you can do yourself—such as painting, making curtains, or stripping floors—will translate into big savings. There's only one warning here: the reason we pay outsiders to do these jobs is that they are time-consuming and tedious. You won't be saving much if you get bored halfway through painting your apartment! (Note: although you can do carpentry and sewing work yourself if you are handy, you will generally need an electrician to do wiring.)

BUYING A SOFA

If you shop around, you should be able to find a good sofa for less than $1,000.

TIP

"Fabric is the most important aspect of the English style. The English palette calls for faded summer colors and pastel; none of the patterns should be bright or harsh. In England, if a fabric looks too new, it's often dipped in tea to 'age' it."

—Lynn Levenberg

The more popular styles are often on sale for less than $700. These sofas are moderately priced because they are popular styles and are mass produced. A department store sofa should last about seven years. Usually it's not worth the cost of upholstering to cover them.

Custom-made sofas

"Before spending more than $1,500 on a ready-made sofa," advises Lynn Levenberg, "consider a custom-made sofa. You may get better construction, better filling, and more detailing. You will also have the luxury of specifying the fabric, the length, the height, and any finishing touches (such as trim or skirt style) that you want. These sofas will last twenty years and they are a great investment in comfort and style."

When shopping for a custom-made sofa, show the upholsterer a picture of the sofa you want, give measurements, and have a swatch of the fabric with you. Always get at least two estimates before making a decision.

Convertible Sleep Sofas

The price range for a department store sleep sofa with a double-size mattress runs from $600 to $800. As with any

DECORATING DILEMMA

"I Want a Royal Bed— But Not for a King's Ransom!"

Bette Landers is engaged to be married in four months. Her apartment is bigger than that of her fiancé, Barney, and he will move into her place by the time they are married. Bette's apartment is very nicely furnished, but she wants to spruce it up. "I don't really need any major changes or expensive new furniture. I just want to freshen the apartment before Barney moves in."

DESIGNER: STANLEY HURA

Bette and Barney are going to England for their honeymoon. They are spending one night at a castle. Bette had a brochure in which she'd found a picture of a beautiful baronial bedroom with a crown canopy bed.

We decided to adapt the crown style to her bedroom and her budget by making the crown canopy with a pair of ruffled priscilla-type curtains that hang from a "coronet" bracketed to the wall behind the bed (see box). The fabric behind the bed is a sheet that matches the bed pattern and is gathered onto a curtain rod under the valance. Tiebacks hold the curtain in place.

The cost of this project was very low because Bette did the sewing and Barney did the installation.

Curtains (one pair)	$45
Sheet (king size)	30
Curtain rods, velcro, chipboard, hardware	18
	$93

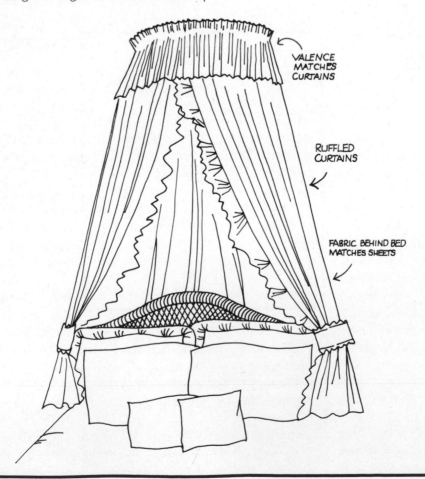

VALENCE MATCHES CURTAINS

RUFFLED CURTAINS

FABRIC BEHIND BED MATCHES SHEETS

HOW TO...
Make a Crown Canopy

First, cut a "coronet" to your desired dimensions out of chipboard, foam board, or plywood. Paint the board before you mount it. When you bracket the coronet to the wall, add small wood blocks between the board and the ceiling. These will help the fabric drape properly.

Mount the curtains to the board by shirring the fabric onto a strip of velcro, then tacking the opposite strip of velcro to the board. This makes it easy to remove the

SMALL WOOD SPACERS BETWEEN FORM AND CEILING HELP FABRIC DRAPE PROPERLY

CHIPBOARD, FOAM BOARD OR PLYWOOD HALF ROUND CUT TO MEASURE AT LUMBER YARD

CUT TO YOUR DIMENSIONS

curtains for cleaning. When hanging the curtains, note that most ready-made varieties are 6'9" long. If you want extra length, cut off the portion behind the bed that won't show anyhow.

---

upholstered furniture, the price will be higher if you don't select the standard coverings or if you choose a style with more detailing. Most sleep sofas have a five-inch-thick foam mattress, which can be quite comfortable. However, if this will be your main bed, you might consider a model that includes a box spring or thicker foam mattress.

When shopping for a sleep sofa, note whether it opens and closes easily and whether the mattress is comfortable. Also note whether the sofa cushions lie flat when the bed is closed. Some closed sleep sofas leave an unsightly gap between the mattress backing and the cushions.

The Lawson Sofa

The Lawson sofa is available for $700 and up, and has a useful chameleon quality. It blends with contemporary and yet it's ideal for traditional rooms. It's a favorite choice of decorators

when they are creating rooms with an English feeling, particularly when it is slipcovered or upholstered in a soft floral print.

BUYING ANTIQUES

We've all heard stories of those who find Tiffany lamps at a barn sale, but you can consider those as apocryphal

yarns. When buying antiques, you almost always get what you're paying for. If something is priced too much below the market value, it should be viewed with suspicion.

A piece needn't be museum quality to be a real treasure. An old chair, a graceful vase from the 1920s, a nineteenth-century painting are the types of items that can still be found at flea markets and secondhand shops. One of the best buys in home furnishings is older kilims (see Chapter 6). Many are still available for less than $1,000. They are decorative and will probably continue to increase in value.

Designers agree that antiques are a good investment. Gerald Kuhn points out that "antiques are always a better buy than expensive reproductions, which are worth half of what you paid the minute they leave the showroom. Your antique may not double in value overnight—but it will probably become more valuable over time."

Howard Kaplan adds, "When you buy an antique from a dealer, you are paying retail and your price includes the cost of selling it. There is a time lag before the piece begins to increase in value. It can be as short as a year or as long as ten years, depending on the piece."

Now that you've roughed out a budget, let's tackle the next big issue: planning your space.

PLAN YOUR SPACE

STARTING OUT

You define yourself aesthetically just as you define yourself personally: by your quirks, likes, and dislikes. When you know that you hate pastels, love antiques, and would give up dessert for a year in order to buy a pre-Columbian statue, then you've started the decorating process.

However, we are often unrealistic in our expectations. We're disappointed when we don't intuitively know what's right. It seems as if perfect taste is a trait with which The Chosen Ones were born. Didactic though it may sound, there's only one way to develop a strong sense of style, and that is by becoming knowledgeable enough to be discerning.

You learn the "tricks of the trade" by studying how others pull together a room. We are constantly surrounded by ideas—when we choose to see them. Look at the lighting in your favorite restaurant and you'll probably discover that it's at the perfect height; notice the way clothes are presented in your favorite boutique and you'll get storage ideas. Decorating magazines and department store model rooms are two terrific sources for ideas.

"The best way to use decorating magazines is to pick out rooms that you instinctively like—and then try to figure out what attracted you to that room," says Kim Freeman. "Was it the color, the furniture arrangement, the lavish use of patterns? It's important to be analytical and isolate particular ideas from the overall design."

Department stores with good model rooms also tend to have excellent decorating departments. You might want to check into the possibility of working with the store's decorators. Generally, there's no cost for the decorating service when you buy your furniture through the store.

When you start shopping for furniture, always go the the best stores and look at the most expensive magazines. This will train your eye to recognize fine materials and good proportions.

Once you know what the best originals look like, then you'll be able to spot the best copies!

Since you're now on the verge of becoming your own decorator, you should begin shopping the same way that professionals do. "Decorators know how easy it is to forget the exact dimensions of a room or the length of a sofa," says Lynn Levenberg, "So we write everything down. Almost every decorator keeps a special notebook for each job and a shopping bag with samples and swatches."

DON'T LEAVE HOME WITHOUT IT!

Lynn Levenberg suggests that you take the following items along when you shop:

• *A floorplan.* You need to know exactly where the radiator is, how long the sofa wall is, and whether there's space in the hallway for the credenza that's on sale.

• *Polaroids or photos of furniture you already own* or have recently purchased. On the back of the photograph, note the dimensions of the piece or pieces.

• *Swatches of fabric and wallpaper.* If you've been considering several patterns, keep small pieces of each stapled to a manila folder. This will serve as a reference when you are looking at rugs or shopping for anything where color coordination is important.

• *Paint chips.* Even decorators don't remember the exact shade. Was the color slightly grayish or more pinkish? If you have the chip, you'll know!

THE IMPORTANCE OF FLOORPLANS

Many beginners skip the most crucial step in decorating: they start buying furniture without having a floorplan. This is asking for trouble. Even professionals wouldn't try guessing the size of the room or the size of the wall against which a piece of furniture is to be placed.

If you have chosen a pleasing color scheme, then doing a floorplan will put you in a fail-safe position in decorating. You will be on the winning side of a bet that no piece will be too large or too small, and that each will fit into the room without overpowering the pieces around it. A floorplan is like insurance—yet many people worry more about the accessories or the color scheme than whether their furniture will work in the room.

The reason for this, I believe, is that making a floorplan seems like excess paperwork—something like cutting out dolls. Or, conversely, it seems too complicated—the kind of thing that only professionals do. But it's not make-work, it's not complicated (see box)—and odds are you'll even find it fun to do.

HOW TO... Make a Floorplan

Start with graph paper. Trace the plan from the landlord onto the graph paper. Establish the scale. The easiest is ¼ inch = 1 foot. For instance, if one inch on your floorplan equals four feet, then a six-foot-long sofa will take up one and a half inches on your plan.

Before committing yourself to your landlord's floorplan, check it against your apartment. Get out a tape measure or ruler and see if the dimensions are accurate. If they are not, you'll need to make adjustments.

Of course, in some buildings, the landlords don't supply floorplans. What then? Start from scratch. Granted, it is more time-consuming to have to measure the walls and radiators yourself, to note where the pillars are placed and how deep they are, etc. But you'll find the extra time you spend at this stage is actually an added blessing, for you'll be focusing on the space and thinking about it. Be sure to measure everything—the depth of the refrigerator, the length and width of the hallway. You'll hate yourself if you see a great sale on small rugs that you can't take advantage of because you don't have the dimensions of your foyer!

Do your initial floorplan in pencil so you can erase. When it's absolutely right, trace over it. (Remember the child's trick of tracing pictures by putting the original and copy sheet on the window?) Now you can have a dozen copies made, or keep working in pencil and erasing as you plan your furniture. When you've finished your floorplan, you'll be amazed by how much you didn't notice when you first looked at your space.

EXPERIMENT WITH YOUR FLOORPLAN

The beauty of a floorplan is that it lets you visualize different arrangements of furniture without backbreaking work or costly mistakes. Try the following exercises to get a sense of the most workable plan for your apartment. By playing with ideas, you'll begin to see how you want your space to work.

First, trace the furniture shapes on the following pages and cut out a sofa, chairs, tables, a rug, or whatever furniture most suits your needs. Now try putting the sofa in the middle of the long wall with the two chairs on either side of the sofa. Where would you put the dining table? Instead of a rectangular dining table, would a square one fit in better? Would it be more interesting if the two chairs were opposite the sofa?

Try putting the sofa with its back against the window. Rearrange the chairs and find an ideal place for the dining table. Does this layout look more open? Does it leave you space for a desk and bookshelves? Try putting the sofa at an angle.

Try out rug sizes. Would you like a rug in the conversation area? Pencil in a 3' x 6' size rug that goes under the front legs of the sofa. Does this look right? Or is it a bit skimpy? Try a 6' x 9' size. Now pencil in coffee tables and end tables, plus chairs around the dining table. Can you begin visualizing the room? As you look at the plan, would you like to add another rug under the dining table? What size should it be?

What are the other changes you might make? Would you prefer a modular sofa? Try it. Most sectionals are composed of three-foot-square modules. Try doing an L shape; then try a U shape.

LEARN FROM THE EXPERTS

The way a decorator approaches planning space is an intrinsic part of his or her design philosophy. Some gravitate toward openness and others create small, intimate seating areas; some start by planning the storage and functional aspects of the apartment and others start by imagining what you'll see the moment you enter the living room door.

Below you'll find thoughts on planning from the pros. See whether their approaches might work for your space—you'll find some terrific pointers here.

Paul Shafer

"You are always re-evaluating a design—going over it again and again. It takes a long time until each piece has its own slot. It's a process: you have an idea and then you think about it and refine it. Once you know where you want a divider to be, then you have to decide whether you want to see through it, or have it completely block off the view.

"Most people get concrete too soon. The design should emerge in a logical way. The real starting point is to list all the things that you really want or need from the room. I find that people restrict themselves unnecessarily: 'I need a desk,' they say, 'but I guess I

can only have a desk that's two feet long.' You don't know if that's so until you've worked out a floorplan."

Howard Kaplan

"The way to get the most of out of a small space is by not restricting the rooms to their traditional divisions—living room and bedroom. Both rooms should be used interchangeably. There's no reason that you can't have a small table and chairs in the bedroom.

> **TIP** ▽
>
> *Here are three dead giveaways that indicate your floorplan isn't working:*
> *• When your guests rearrange the furniture during a party so they can create a more comfortable conversational area.*
> *• When they pull over an end table or coffee table so they can find a place for their drinks or ashtrays.*
> *• When the telephone and Kleenex are on the floor and your books are piled on a chair.*
> *—Lynn Levenberg*

You should be able to have breakfast in front of the window of your bedroom rather than cramming yourself into a little tiny dining area. You should be able to write a letter, play cards, or work in either room. And you should feel comfortable having guests in both rooms.

"Ideally, both spaces will feel like a sitting room or a den. This means choosing furniture that doesn't look like only bedroom or living room furni-

ture, so that you can continue the style throughout. For instance, an armoire might be better than a small bedroomy-looking chest of drawers; a sleigh bed looks more like a sofa than a place to sleep; a small pine writing table is equally right in a living room or bedroom.

"When you are decorating a small apartment, you have to be absolutely ruthless in your decisions. Spotlighting one perfect flower is pretentious and a waste of space when you have to give up a whole table top to it.

Here are Kaplan's pointers on how to get the most out of your space:
• In modern apartments where there's a wall of windows, many people tend to shy away from putting the sofa at the end of the room. This often means that the last five feet of space is wasted—the only time you use it is when you go over to put the blinds down. With the sofa at the end of the room, the space seems longer. The eye tends to stop at the seating area. In a twenty-four foot room with a seven-foot foyer, the sofa will be thirty-one feet from the door. You have defined the space at its outer boundaries rather than at the center of the room.
• Consider building in a window seat in front of the windows. The base would give you a long storage box. Have a mattress upholstered or slipcovered to match pillows, and staple the same fabric over the base.
• Instead of two little end tables, which is very ordinary, use a long writing table at one side of the sofa.
• If you have room in the bedroom, try putting your bed at a 45° angle to the corner. It's unexpected and gives the room an interesting look.
• Try something different. For instance, if you have a nice window, you may want to put the dining table there. It may seem like a long way from the kitchen, but it's easy enough to manage serving if you use a little cart.

DECORATING DILEMMA

veniently located. "I don't mind living in one room if it's well laid out," she says. "But I am bothered by the boredom of being in the same space every day, season after season. Without a second room, there's no way to have a change of scenery."

When Your Summer Place Is Your Winter Place

When a freelance fabric designer works at home, she has two major problems: light and storage.

Designs for sheets and fabrics are first sketched on drawing paper, then they are traced and retraced, adjustments made, the scale changed, and each line checked again and again until the design is perfected. The tracings are sequential, and if any of the drawings are lost, the whole series has to be reconstructed.

After the designs are perfected, the colors are chosen. There are literally thousands of variations of any one color, and to choose exactly the right shade the designer must have an absolutely perfect eye—and perfect light.

"I need a place to store my drawings and I want to work in natural light," Rhonda Baron told her decorator.

Rhonda had chosen a studio apartment in a good neighborhood instead of a larger place that was less con-

DESIGNER: STANLEY HURA

Because she works at home, Rhonda spends more time in her apartment than most people, and we decided that it was a priority to help her find a way to relieve the day-to-day sameness of studio apartment living. Since she couldn't afford a second room, we decided to give her two looks for the same room.

The bookshelf on the long wall was constructed with enough depth for drawer and file space. The drawers are inexpensive white plastic modular units that hold her drawings; two file cabinets hold her papers. The drawers and files are interspersed with baskets, which look decorative, but they are also for storage: one of the baskets holds lingerie and the others have fabric swatches.

Rhonda's worktable is near the window, which gives

SUMMER

FOLDING SCREENS ON ROLLERS

STRAW MAT RUG

BED ALSO SERVES AS SOFA

BASKETS USED FOR STORAGE

DECORATING DILEMMA

her ideal lighting conditions. Rather than using conventional curtains, we constructed folding screens from hollow doors. The doors are hinged together and there are rollers on the bottom that make it easy to move them back and forth.

Although Rhonda doesn't have immediate plans for moving, she didn't want any built-ins or furniture that couldn't be moved to another apartment. She was equally adamant about wanting to be able to change this apartment at will. The solution was in making dramatic changes in the layout—other than the bookshelves—and changing the fabrics for summer and winter.

For summer, Rhonda chose a light-colored fabric and had a slipcover made for the base of the bed, which also serves as a sofa. The box springs are on the floor and the slipcover is snapped on and off. The mattress covering is a matching sheet fabric. The panels of the screen in front of the window are slipcovered in a coordinating pattern, so they can be easily removed for washing.

The floorplan changes radically between winter and summer. In the summer, Rhonda puts her sofa in the middle of the room at an angle. A bolster divides the width of the mattress so it becomes a two-sided seating piece. An inexpensive straw mat picks up the light color scheme and makes the apartment look like a beach house.

In the winter, Rhonda pushes the bed against the wall and recovers the mattress, box springs, pillows, and window screen in a dark-colored print. A geometric Dhurrie rug in the middle of the room with rich winter reds and greens changes the summer house to a cozy retreat.

Even the dining area is given a winter warmth. Pillows that match the sofa are tied onto the spindleback chairs. The placemats and napkins are part of the changeover look. With just a few adjustments in fabric and floorplan, Rhonda has the luxury of changing her apartment without having to change her furniture.

SHADES, PILLOWS AND SLIPCOVERS MADE FROM MATCHING FABRIC

WINTER

GEOMETRIC DHURRIE RUG

DECORATING DILEMMA

"I Like Entertaining—Sometimes."

A friend who often entertained asked her designer to suggest a layout that would be appropriate for both everyday use and socializing. She wanted to close off the sleeping area when she had company, and she wanted a divider between the dining area and living room. She wanted to be able to keep extra plates and glasses near the table, and wanted the divider to block the view of the dining table after dinner. In addition, she was on a strict budget. "Nothing custom and no built-ins," she warned.

DESIGNER: TIM MEIER

Meier's solution was a buffet/bookshelf combination. The lower cabinets are closed and can accommodate dishes and serving pieces. The top of the buffet is used for serving, and bookshelves hold the stereo equipment, plants, and a small collection of first edition Victorian children's books.

Vertical blinds cover the windows and also provided a solution to the problem of closing off the sleeping area. "I don't want anything as elaborate as sliding doors," she said, so Meier had a track installed and hung vertical blinds across the sleeping alcove. When they are drawn closed, they suggest a continuation of the window.

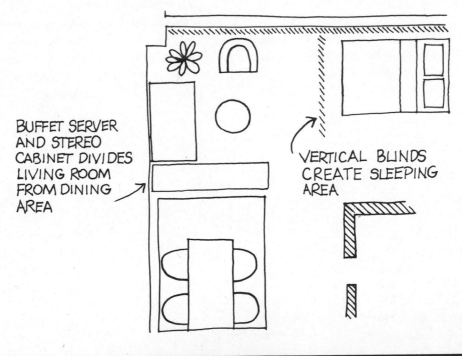

BUFFET SERVER AND STEREO CABINET DIVIDES LIVING ROOM FROM DINING AREA

VERTICAL BLINDS CREATE SLEEPING AREA

Gerald Kuhn

"When you are doing a floorplan, always start with the biggest pieces first. Those are the pieces that are hardest to handle. Incidentals like lamps and side tables are not as important as the size and location of a sofa, a buffet, or a dining table. When the big pieces are right, you can always find a place for a side table or an accessory.

"If you are unsure about how the furniture will work in the room, then go beyond your floorplan. Take measurements of the pieces that you intend to buy, particularly the large pieces like the sofa and dining table. Then outline the shapes with masking tape on the floor and wall to show you how much space each piece will take up.

"Furniture can seem more interesting if you bring it away from the wall to create an island in the middle of the room. You might also want to try turning the furniture and rug on an angle.

"People often sacrifice too much for the view. They turn the furniture toward the window and all you see when you walk in the room is the backs of everything. This is very boring. The view will always be there. And you can always take a cup of coffee over and stand by the window!"

Ronald Bricke

"There are two universal myths. One is a fireplace and the other is a view. When you have guests or you are by yourself, you don't sit there glaring at the fireplace! You're aware of it when you walk into the room, but afterwards you forget it when you are reading or watching television.

"A view creates ambience. You get drama, suspense, and openness in the room, but you're not clamped onto that sight. When your eye is at rest, it's nice to look up and see a vista, but I don't feel the need to design a room so that I'm always looking out of the window or staring into the fireplace."

"All good floorplans are balanced. Although we tend to think of balance as having masses opposite each other, in a room this may actually unbalance or crowd the space.

"There's a formula that usually works in doing floor plans: think in terms of the triangle. Start with the largest piece of furniture, which is usually the sofa. Then take your next biggest object—let's say it's a desk—and then the dining table. These three pieces will be the ballast for the smaller pieces, such as the end tables and chairs. Setting the three big pieces at

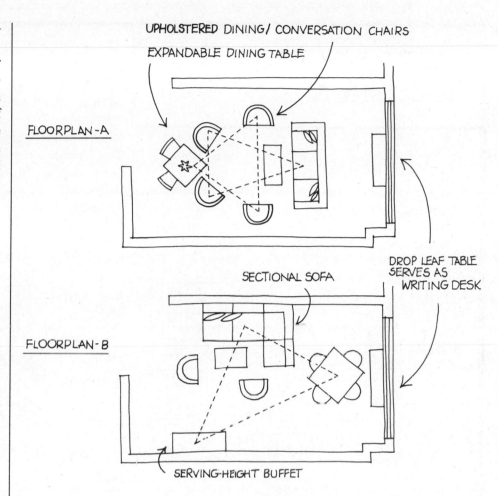

FLOORPLAN-A

UPHOLSTERED DINING/ CONVERSATION CHAIRS
EXPANDABLE DINING TABLE

DROP LEAF TABLE SERVES AS WRITING DESK

SECTIONAL SOFA

FLOORPLAN-B

SERVING-HEIGHT BUFFET

the corners of your triangle eliminates the problem of heavy pieces being opposite each other and throwing off the balance of the room." (See floorplan A above.)

In a perfectly balanced floor plan, there might be two triangles intersecting (see floorplan B above). Bricke calls this his "Foolproof Floorplan" for a rectangular room.

"There's a feeling of spaciousness in floorplan A because all the furniture is away from the wall and there's room behind you wherever you are seated. But floorplan B also provides great design."

The choice of a square dining table is the key to making both rooms work.

"It doesn't read as a dining table even though it can be expanded," says Bricke. Two of the four dining chairs in floorplan A are upholstered and can be turned toward the sofa to create a conversational area for six. The other two dining chairs are smaller and unobtrusive.

"You could never achieve this much openness in a small space if you used a rectangular table. They are unnecessarily long and obtrusive and you end up using half your space for dining. With a small square or round table at one end, you're using the full room as your living room."

In both floorplans, a drop leaf table at the rear is used as a combination

DECORATING DILEMMA

The Odd Couple

Leonard Barkin, twenty-two, and David Aronson, twenty-one, refer to themselves as the "odd couple." They knew each other casually at Yale and recently decided to share a one-bedroom apartment in Manhattan.

"I was living in Brooklyn and Len had a slummy studio downtown," David explains. "Neither of us could afford a first-rate place on his own, so we decided to pool our resources. This is temporary for both of us—maybe a year at the outside."

On the surface, the two men share little in common.

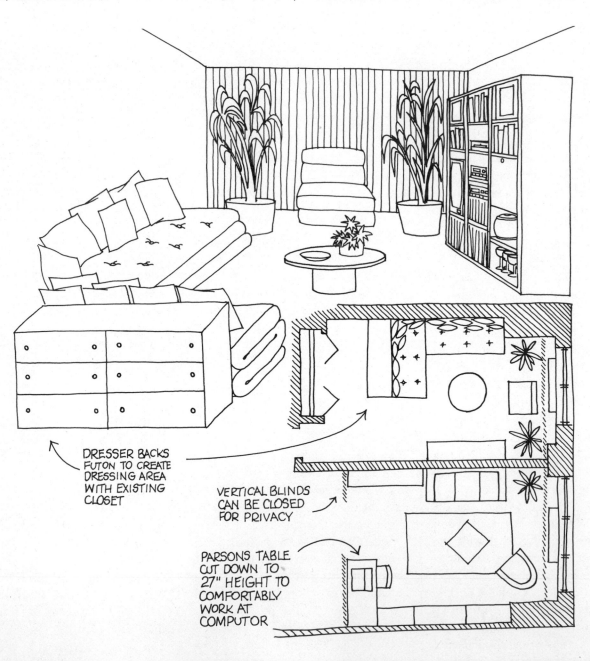

DRESSER BACKS FUTON TO CREATE DRESSING AREA WITH EXISTING CLOSET

VERTICAL BLINDS CAN BE CLOSED FOR PRIVACY

PARSONS TABLE CUT DOWN TO 27" HEIGHT TO COMFORTABLY WORK AT COMPUTOR

DECORATING DILEMMA

Leonard dates constantly and is an admitted non-intellectual. "I care more about mood lights than reading lights," he told their designer.

David, on the other hand, is a homebody. He loves to cook and he has an extraordinary collection of jazz albums and tapes. His newest passion is a home computer. "I adjust every program and I play with the thing constantly. I need a place for the manuals and a computer table."

Since Leonard needed more privacy and David needed more space, Len took the bedroom and David chose the living room. They each bought their own furniture so when they split up, each will have one completely furnished room to take with him or sell to the next tenant.

DESIGNER: TIM MEIER

Both men have very good taste and an excellent sense of where to invest their money in the apartment. Since they don't expect to be living together permanently, it was important to choose a color that would work not only with their furniture but also with the next tenant's. We chose gray—a dark shade for Len's room and a lighter color for the living room—because gray is a beautiful background for almost any color.

Their only nonremovable investment was in vertical blinds. We chose black aluminum verticals, which are a smart-looking counterpoint to the gray walls.

Both men wanted carpeting for the floor, but they weren't very particular about whether it was of the finest quality. "I don't expect to live with it forever," said Len. We found a remnant large enough to go almost wall to wall in both rooms. Instead of having it permanently installed as wall-to-wall carpeting, we had the edges finished so it could be laid like a rug.

David's major concern was that the living room wouldn't be private. The solution was to install black vertical blinds across the front half of the room. When they aren't needed, they are left open and pushed against the walls. When it's necessary to close the space off, the verticals completely seal his area from view and become the equivalent of a sleek ebony wall from either side.

Instead of buying an expensive computer table, David cut down the legs of a Parsons table to twenty-seven inches—the recommended height for typing. The printer and manual fit neatly on the bookshelves next to the table, with enough space left over for his stereo equipment, tapes, and records.

Len's room is basically all seating and lounging. He chose futon beds and futon-styled chairs, which have a casual look and are excellent for sleeping. The low dresser behind the futons creates a dressing area by the closet.

The track lighting was installed in two horizontal strips so that the spots could be focused on each of the objects in the room—the plants, the pictures over the sofa, and toward the bookshelves. The track lighting is on a rheostat so that Len can dim the lights to a nightclub low.

Six months after the job was completed, both men report the apartment is working superbly for them. They are particularly pleased with the convenience of being able to close the living room off when necessary. "We have all the financial advantages of living together and most of the privacy of living alone," says David. "This arrangement could last for longer than either of us thought possible!"

---

writing and desk space. "Drop leaf tables work wonderfully," says Bricke, "because you can use the back portion for books and papers and then flip up the end to use for writing without having to clear away the whole table."

Drop leaf tables are also very handy in the bedroom. "You don't have to clear the whole side table for a place to put the Sunday paper!"

In a well-conceived floorplan, every piece of furniture is carefully selected.

Sometimes there are trade-offs. In deciding whether to use a modular unit or a traditional sofa, Bricke points out that a "modular unit sometimes gives

(Continued on page 68)

DECORATING DILEMMA

Same Space, Different Place

Although they lived in the same building and took the same elevator every day, Andrea, Nick, and Betty and Al were barely on nodding terms with each other until there was a leak that turned into a flood and ruined the furniture in their three apartments. They met when it became necessary to band together to sue for damages. When the landlord settled out of court, they each decided to use the money to furnish their apartments from scratch.

Although their apartments are exactly alike—a 700-square-foot L-shaped studio—their needs are totally different, as they explained to their designer.

Andrea

Andrea, twenty-eight, is a trainee with a major cosmetics company. She started as a makeup consultant at department stores and now the company has put her in charge of three of their major accounts. Her next promotion will be a transfer to another city.

"I know I'll be moving within the next two years and I want furniture that will look good in any type of apartment," she said. "I don't want to invest in painting the wall or refinishing the floors."

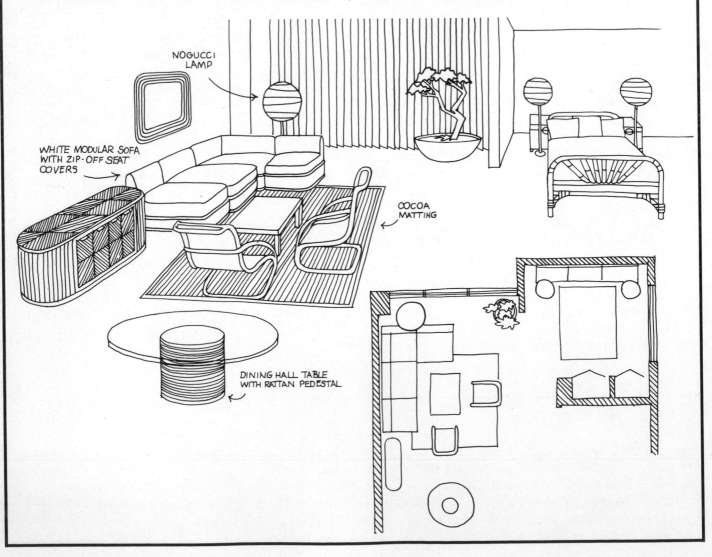

NOGUCCI LAMP

WHITE MODULAR SOFA WITH ZIP-OFF SEAT COVERS

COCOA MATTING

DINING HALL TABLE WITH RATTAN PEDESTAL

DECORATING DILEMMA

Nick

Nick plans to be a millionaire before he's thirty-five. He's a lean, handsome sandy blond who dresses impeccably and is already starting to make it big in insurance. He uses the apartment to entertain clients and he wants it to be very polished.

"I'll probably buy a larger place in the next two or three years, but I'd like this apartment to have a very finished look. Good furniture is a good investment for me. It is an image-builder."

Betty and Al

Betty and Al were high-school sweethearts who married the summer they graduated from college. Betty's parents are wholesale florists and she grew up in the business. She and Al took advantage of their connections and started a chain of street-stand floral kiosks. The business is fabulously successful—but it doesn't leave much time for a home life: they are out before dawn selecting flowers and they do the books at night. "We don't need a larger place until we start a family, but we

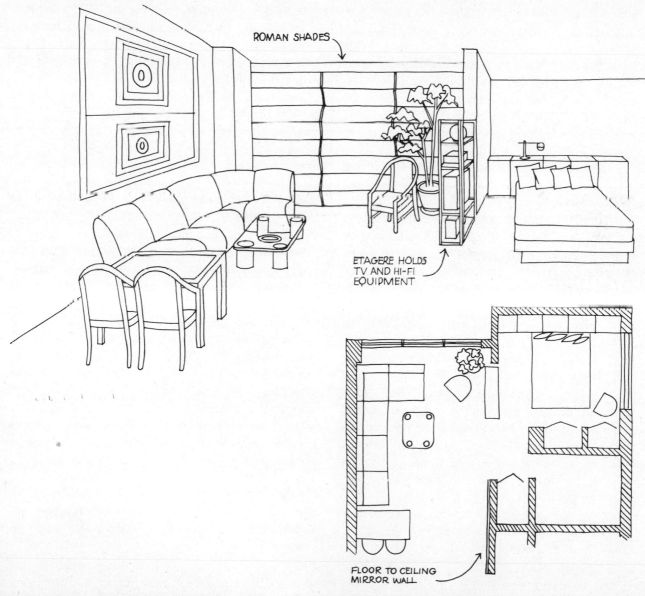

ROMAN SHADES

ETAGERE HOLDS
TV AND HI-FI
EQUIPMENT

FLOOR TO CEILING
MIRROR WALL

DECORATING DILEMMA

do want to be very comfortable here," they said. "We're traditionalists at heart, and we want furniture with character."

DESIGNER: RICHARD KNAPPLE

Andrea

Andrea's life is in a state of flux. She doesn't know how much longer she'll be in New York or where she might be moving next. Some people might be edgy about this situation, but Andrea sees the open-ended possibilities as exciting. We furnished her apartment with rattan pieces that will mix with any future style she selects for her next place. Rattan is always a good choice when you're starting out. Her major expenditure was for the modular sofa—a sectional that will give her flexibility when she moves. The sectional has zip-off seat covers so that she can change her color scheme by changing the covers.

We chose white walls because Andrea doesn't want to repaint when she moves. Instead of being boring, we used white as a color with dramatic impact. To make white a strong statement, you must use a lot of it. For Andrea, we emphasized white by using it as the color for the canvas slipcovers and the coffee table. White is perfect with rattan, cocoa matting, and natural materials. They always feel right together.

The Noguchi lamp is so stylish that it almost takes the place of art in a contemporary room. This lamp is widely available and it's a true classic. Andrea couldn't afford an expensive painting for over the sofa, so instead of second-rate artwork, we bought a rattan mirror that can be moved to another wall when she can finally afford a painting; or the mirror can be used in the bedroom of her next place. A mirror with a good-looking frame never goes to waste; there's always a wall for it.

Although Andrea isn't very domestic, she needs a dinner table for the few occasions when she has company. We chose a rattan pedestal with a round glass top that can be used as a hall table when it stands alone or as a dinner table with the four folding chairs in the closet. When Andrea moves, the pedestal base can be used as a sculpture stand or as an end table or as a base for a larger dinner table if a bigger piece of glass is used.

Nick

Nick's taste is more dramatic than Andrea's. He wants people to think he spent a lot of money. We created an expensive look in his place using the color scheme as much as the furniture. We used taupe—a brownish gray—in the carpeting, the walls, and the furniture. This is a very sophisticated color and it looks quite good with shiny finishes, such as glass and steel.

Nick loves the feeling of polished metal and the pared-down, low-lined European type of modular systems you expect to see in Milan. This furniture is very elegant, but it can also seem cold unless it is warmed with carpeting and a color on the wall. Carpeting ties glass, metal, and sleek lines together and gives them warmth. In this monochromatic color scheme, we selected carpeting of a darker shade than the wall. This is more interesting than matching the colors exactly.

We used black as the accent color. This is a very chic color scheme and gives a room the urbane elegance Nick wants. We used black on the table top and in the chairs. The two chairs by the dining table match the two side chairs in the living room. This is a small apartment and we didn't want to introduce too many different styles—the room would become busy-looking.

Instead of using a wall, we used a black metal and glass étagère to visually divide the space between the living area and the alcove. It adds an element of interest without crowding the room. We were very careful to keep this space uncluttered and open. A mirror on the short wall creates the impression of a window and adds a touch of glitter to the room.

In keeping with the sleek feeling of the room, the windows are covered with a taupe brown pleated sunscreen. It hangs from ceiling to floor and covers the radiator.

DECORATING DILEMMA

Betty and Al

Betty and Al presented the most interesting and, perhaps, rewarding challenge because they wanted the feeling of a home in a standard studio apartment. They both love wood and earthy textures. Although they are buying all their furniture at the same time, they don't want everything to match and look as if it came off the same assembly line. Their ideal is a home in which beautiful pieces have been collected over time.

The living room was divided from the bedroom by a wall which Betty and Al had installed earlier. Although the bedroom area is very small, they felt it gave them a measure of privacy, which is important to a couple. The entire apartment was painted an eggshell shade, which is a very good color with traditional furnishings. It's also near enough to white so that you won't have to paint over it when you move out.

In the living room, we used rag rugs to create the two areas—the dining/desk area near the entrance and the living area in the rear of the room. Rag rugs are terrific when you're trying to find a color scheme—there are always at least two colors that you can pull out as your

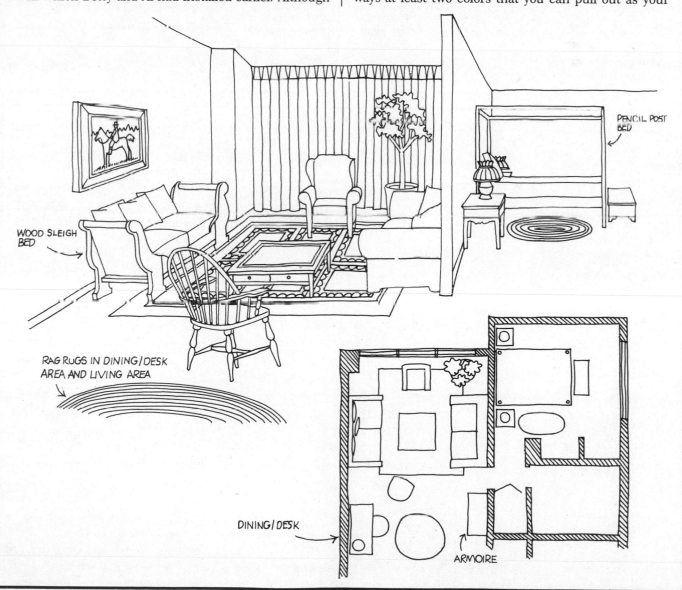

WOOD SLEIGH BED

PENCIL POST BED

RAG RUGS IN DINING/DESK AREA AND LIVING AREA

DINING/DESK

ARMOIRE

dominant colors. The colors we used were red and blue.

We used two very interesting pieces of furniture in the living area, a wood sleigh bed and a wingback chair (see the $avvy $hopper on page 49). Both of these styles have a lot of character. The sleigh bed costs about the same as a sleep sofa—about $900—but it is more interesting. Although Betty and Al like traditional styling, they wanted the apartment done with a light touch. We gave the room an upbeat feeling with our choice of fabrics, a red-and-blue plaid on the wing chair and blue denim on the sofa opposite the sleigh bed. This sofa is a very ordinary style. Every piece of furniture needn't be unusual. That makes the apartment look like a showroom.

An armoire was their biggest luxury in the living room—a tall, plain two-door Early American style. The wood adds warmth to the room and the height adds interest. An armoire is always a special piece of furniture. It's something that people notice and remember. Though they tend to be more expensive than ordinary chests, they are worth more in terms of showmanship.

In the bedroom, a pencil-post bed turns the tiny little space into an interesting room. The bed has a lot of style and it mixes well with contemporary or traditional pieces. It's more like a piece of sculpture than a piece of furniture.

a cleaner line because there's nothing to break it up or separate it. It looks more serene than a sofa and two chairs would, but it might also look less interesting.

"It's a mistake to think that modulars solve all seating problems. Sometimes the sheer mass of so much fabric and color on one side of the room will make the space seem top-heavy. You'll need an important piece on the opposite side to balance the modular unit."

SHOULD YOU DIVIDE YOUR SPACE?

To divide or not to divide? That is the question in a studio apartment. We often start with traditional assumptions: that a bed should be closed off from view, that an office should be separate from the living area, that it's more stylish to have separate rooms. But a studio apartment is a nontraditional space and you may want to examine each as-

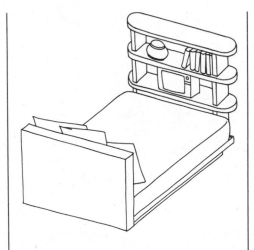

sumption before continuing. Does it really matter if your guests see the bed? Is it really necessary that your office be closed off?

You don't have to be a mathematician to realize that every time you divide a space, you have two smaller spaces. Is this really what you want? Or would you rather be able to see the whole expanse of your apartment from every corner?

Before you can answer these questions, you should think in terms

of organizing the room for your needs. Partitions are usually major changes—and major purchases. Because you will have to live with any decision you make about dividing your space for a long time, think the project through carefully. How do you want your apartment to function? Answering the following questions will help you to determine your needs:

• Do you want a sleeping area that is completely closed off with a permanent division? Or would you be willing to separate an alcove without building a permanent wall?

"Sometimes people assume they should divide an apartment because they are used to having a separate bedroom. But you can separate an alcove without building a permanent wall," says Tim Meier. "For instance, you could have a bookcase at the end of the bed that would hold the television and be decorative on both sides." Formica shelving units with rounded edges have a very finished look; they also come in a wide range of colors.

DECORATING DILEMMA

Divide and Conquer

Under a pseudonym, Steven Brandon, thirty-eight, is a successful science fiction writer. It's a passion as much as a profession, and his enormous collection of books is an integral part of his life. Of necessity, his days are solitary, but in the evening, he loves to entertain. He gives dinner parties several times a week and encourages a constant stream of friends to drop by for cocktails or a late-night drink.

As much as he enjoys the company, Steve doesn't want his office or his bedroom to be public property. This presented a problem. He has a one-bedroom apartment in a beautiful old brownstone. The living room is graciously proportioned, with a lovely marble fireplace; the second room measures a long, narrow 8' × 16', usually a space just large enough to serve as a bedroom. To use the room only for sleeping, though, would have meant having the office in the living room.

"When your office is in the living room, people look at your work or disturb your papers. That makes me crazy," he explained to his designers.

Brandon's friends are other successful writers, artists, theatrical people, and architects. He wanted a working environment that he would be proud to show off on occasion. Furthermore, any design solution would have to include his dog, Rigby, an enormous, shaggy American Water Spaniel who will only drink when he's near Brandon. "But he doesn't just drink," says Brandon, "he dunks himself into the bowl and then shakes the water all over everything."

DESIGNERS: PAUL SHAFER AND JEAN WEINER

Sometimes it's necessary to divide a space to make it functional. In this instance, Steve needed the bedroom to work in three different ways: as a study, as a sleeping area, and as a watering spot for his dog. Conventional furniture would have simply crowded such a small space. Our solution was to create three areas which would be completely private from each other.

Having his books, research materials, and typewriter in close proximity was essential for Steve. He has an enormous number of books and he was very particular as to how they were to be stored. He knew what he wanted—down to specifying that there be a space for a large dictionary that could always be left open.

When he works, he doesn't want to look at his bed, and when he is sleeping or watching television, he doesn't want to be confronted with his desk. He likes to watch television in bed, and he needs a light by the bed for reading.

The dog, Rigby, presented as much of a challenge as figuring out how to store 1,000 books. When the dog shakes himself, he creates a veritable fountain. Steve doesn't mind the water, but his publisher hates dripping wet manuscripts.

We divided the space according to use. The area by the window was designed as the office. By adding a wall and building in bookshelves, Steve got almost the equivalent of a library—three walls of books. One shelf was for the open dictionary.

There were still more books left over. To accommodate these, storage columns just deep enough for books were placed in the aisle that faced the door. When you enter, you see lacquered columns rather than the whole room. Each space unfolds as you walk through the area.

The wall that holds the books on the office side holds the television and storage shelves for the bed area on the other side. A wall that serves as a headboard fits exactly against the bed, and the space is cozy with built-in lighting and shelves for his reading materials. On the other side of the headboard, Rigby has his own waterproof space that is Formica-finished and can be washed down. Three feet above Rigby's bowl is a closed closet where Steve can store his extra office supplies.

Lighting is an integral part of this plan. Overhead canopies enclose the lighting fixtures and protect them from view. The fixtures themselves are inexpensive ceramic sockets. The same sockets were used at the top of one of the book columns to create an indirect lighting source.

DECORATING DILEMMA

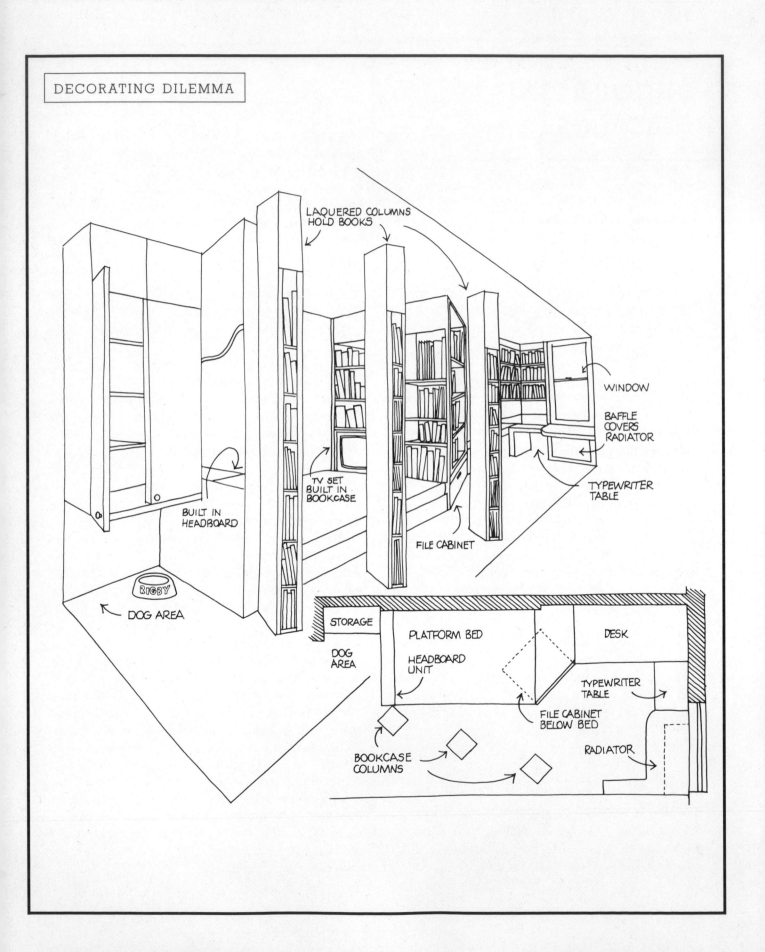

LAQUERED COLUMNS
HOLD BOOKS

WINDOW

BAFFLE
COVERS
RADIATOR

TV SET
BUILT IN
BOOKCASE

TYPEWRITER
TABLE

BUILT IN
HEADBOARD

FILE CABINET

RIGBY

DOG AREA

STORAGE

PLATFORM BED

DESK

DOG
AREA

HEADBOARD
UNIT

TYPEWRITER
TABLE

FILE CABINET
BELOW BED

RADIATOR

BOOKCASE
COLUMNS

• Do you want absolute quiet in a bedroom? You might consider using a wall of plastic, which would allow you to see out but not hear in.

• Will the space seem cramped if you divide it?

• What do you want to see when you come into the apartment? Does it bother you that people can see directly into the living room? Would you prefer creating a small foyer? You might be able to create a visual diversion by simply placing three trees or an étagère to block the view.

• What do you want to see from every area of the apartment? Will it bother you to see the bed from the sofa? To see the kitchen from your desk?

• If you divide up your space, how will you distribute the windows? Will closing off certain areas make them too dark? Do you want to be able to see your view from any area in your apartment?

Decorating is a step-by-step process. You start with the problem—for instance, that you want to divide your space—and then begin to look for solutions. The way your decorators work is by making notes. If they've decided that a visual division is necessary, then their next question is whether it should be partial, such as blocking the view of the alcove with a tree, or a total division, such as a sliding wall. Other options include folding screens and vertical blinds. Don't expect to hit on the perfect solution immediately. Spend some time thinking about what will really work best when you're alone, when you have company, if a lover should move in with you.

When you've finished your floor plan, you're ready to start selecting your colors and choosing your furniture. Good luck!

MAKE THE MOST
OF YOUR WALLS

Walls are the most important element of your apartment. They give your space its character and ambience; they're what people notice first and remember longest. Luckily, even on the most stringent budget you can create beautiful backgrounds with your wall treatments. Paint, for instance, is just about the best buy in decorating: you'll get more mileage for your money by spending $200 on painting than by spending ten times that amount on furniture. Or, with a little extra effort and not too much more cost, you can get the special "luxe" look of wallpaper or fabric wall treatments as well.

Here's how to get a fabulous look for your apartment no matter what wall treatment you choose.

PAINT

If you are on a budget, paint is by far your best decorating choice for a wall treatment (unless there's a definite reason for wallpaper or fabric—more on this later). Paint offers a wide choice of colors and is easy to use. Best of all, it allows you to transform your apartment dramatically with a minimum of effort. A weekend's worth of time is probably all you need to freshen your apartment or provide it with a terrific new look.

Color

One of the great advantages of using paint is that there's almost no color that doesn't already exist or can't be mixed to your specifications. The trick, though, is in deciding which color is right for your apartment.

There are two points where decorators are in total agreement:

• Always use a color on the wall; avoid pure white paint. Blue-white is cold. "Even the lightest pastel will add warmth to a room," says Stanley Hura. "A pure white is too bright. If you want the effect of white, then add just a few drops of a color that you are already using in the room. If your carpeting or sofa is peach, for example, then ask for a few drops of peach to be added to the white you selected. This will warm the room and draw all the colors together."

• Use less color than you think you need. "Pick out a shade that you think you like and then use a shade that is half as intense," says Hura. Colors tend to grow more vivid on the wall. A color that seems moderately lively in a small chip will become positively bold when it's used on a large area. And the larger the area to be painted, the softer the color should be. "If you feel the need for bright colors, then use these in the small spaces of the apartment, such as the kitchen or bathroom," advises Gerald Kuhn.

Making the Most of Color

"Color works best when it's a strong statement," says Ronald Bricke. "You won't get much of a statement with pink walls if the floors are green and the upholstery is blue. You need to have enough of a color so that it becomes a theme. This may mean making a room 75 to 80 percent in one color family. Any color can be glamorous if it's used consistently."

Colors are always relative. They change in relationship to the light and the colors or fabrics they adjoin. This means that you should always plan your scheme in advance. Even if you can't afford to buy a sofa at the same time that you paint the wall, you should try to have a swatch of the fabric you want when you choose the paint.

There's a very nonscientific decorating trick that designers use when they are trying to see if colors and patterns work together. They put all the swatches on the floor and step back and squint. If the colors blend into one another, with no one color standing out, then they begin to feel comfortable with the scheme. If one color stands out, they ask themselves if that's a color that should stand out or whether it is destroying the harmony of the scheme.

Although decorators are the biggest advocates of color, they are the most disciplined in their use of it. When in doubt, they always use less. In an area as large as a wall, even a tint of color will have an effect.

Beware of Dark Colors

Quite often you'll see photographs of beautiful rooms with burgundy, hunter green, or dark brown walls. These rooms invariably look opulent and in-

viting. Dark walls show off artwork and are elegant for entertaining. However, dark colors tend to be a poor choice for a small apartment. They make small rooms seem smaller and they absorb the light. Unless you have other rooms where you can escape the darkness, avoid very deep shades.

An exception to this rule is if you want an extremely elegant look and don't need your apartment to be "homey." In this case, dark lacquered walls can be dramatic and effective.

Planning Your Color Scheme

The easiest, safest, and often best scheme for a small apartment is a monochromatic color scheme, with all the colors in the same color family. "The colors don't have to match exactly. A monochromatic scheme will work beautifully with colors that blend and harmonize," Stanley Hura explains. "With a monochromatic scheme you create a neutral background. Any color becomes a neutral when it is the basic color being used. Other colors appear darker, lighter, or brighter when they are in contrast."

For instance, if you choose a peach scheme, the walls and carpeting throughout can be peach. But each room can be changed subtly by bringing in new shades. In the living room, for instance, mix the peach with plum, melon, and cream in the fabrics in the pillows, draperies, or slipcovers. The peach will become the background color. In the bedroom, all the colors can be in the peach family, creating a warm and intimate feeling. In the den, pick up the peach in a tweed fabric and use a small, patterned rug over the carpeting; in the kitchen, use the peach as a background for pictures and cabinets in crisp white; in the

bathroom, match the peach walls with stylish floral shower curtains.

Decorators have differing opinions on whether a color should be used throughout the apartment. Hura believes it's always wisest to simplify one's scheme and use color to create the feeling of uninterrupted space. "It's jarring to go from a peach room to a brown room. Different colors break the apartment up into a series of tiny areas," he asserts.

The other viewpoint is that color should be used to define space. "If you don't paint the foyer a different color than the living room, you breeze through and don't even realize there was a separate room," says Howard Kaplan. "When the bedroom and living room are the same color, you feel like you're in the same place. There's no reason for this. I always paint or fabric the bedroom a different color. It makes an apartment more interesting."

Which approach feels best for your tastes? Do you like the idea of having your rooms flow together? Will this make it easier for you to plan your color scheme? Or would you prefer to define space with separate colors? Either approach can make an effective decorative statement.

Selecting a Color

Even decorators admit to being confused by the number of color chips that one is confronted with at the paint store. The difficulty in making a selection is often intensified by an incomprehensible numbering system. One company's chip is #721 Sky Blue and another's is #412 Heavenly Blue. They look alike—or so it seems under the fluorescent lights.

Here are tips to help you make failsafe color selections:

• Don't go to the paint shop with a

DECORATING DILEMMA

"Give Me Luxury."

Frank Devon's life sounds like one long vacation: he is the social director for a major steamship company and he sails around the world at least twice a year. "My job is to show people how to have fun," says Devon. He's the perfect person for the job. He speaks four languages and loves being with people. Devon's studio apartment is in midtown Manhattan and he uses it during his brief stints in New York. Even on land, Devon is super sociable and usually has company in for dinner or asks friends over for drinks.

"I use the apartment mostly at night and I'd like it to be very glamorous," he told his designer. Devon's place is an unmemorable L-shaped studio. Its greatest asset is smooth walls and its worst defect is the lack of a foyer or separate entrance hall. Devon would like stylish-looking furniture but he doesn't really care which style. His one specific request is to figure out a way to hang a large painting over the sofa.

"I bought the painting years ago in Barcelona and it's just been leaning against the wall because the beam over the sofa cuts into the space where the picture should hang."

DESIGNER: RONALD BRICKE

If he were rich, Devon would live in a mansion with crystal chandeliers. This is the kind of elegance he wanted on a budget in a studio apartment. Two ways to create glamor instantly is with dark-colored lacquer walls and mirrors; the combination of both together is foolproof. It doesn't really matter whether you choose deepest green, midnight blue, claret, or the chocolate brown that we selected. The darkness of the color is immediately chic—particularly when it's in a high-gloss finish. (Note: if walls aren't very smooth, avoid a gloss finish; it will only highlight the defects.)

The major problem was that the space had no drama—it was like a twenty-eight-foot bowling alley. Instead of going to the expense of building a wall, we decided on a mirrored folding screen on casters, which creates a dining area/foyer and blocks the view from the front door into the living room. It's always best to have a separate dining area, if possible, so that afterwards you don't have to look at the dishes on the table.

The screen was built by a glazier. It has a plywood back which was painted a color to match the wall. A screen adds architectural interest to a space and it's always less expensive than building a wall.

We selected a round table with extensions that can be used as a hall table during the day and a dining table in the evening. The two cane chairs against the wall can be pulled to the table and matched up with the two chairs by the desk. If there's more company, Devon uses

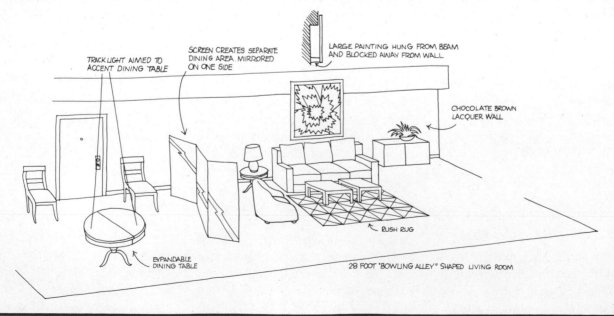

TRACK LIGHT AIMED TO
ACCENT DINING TABLE

SCREEN CREATES SEPARATE
DINING AREA. MIRRORED
ON ONE SIDE

LARGE PAINTING HUNG FROM BEAM
AND BLOCKED AWAY FROM WALL

CHOCOLATE BROWN
LACQUER WALL

RUSH RUG

EXPANDABLE
DINING TABLE

28 FOOT "BOWLING ALLEY" SHAPED LIVING ROOM

folding chairs from the closet and pushes the screen back.

Although the walls are dark, the apartment is airy and unconfining, even during the day. This is because the floors were stripped and refinished with clear polyurethane rather than a dark stain. Light-colored wood floors always make a space look bigger and airier. This impression is heightened when the furniture is chosen to match the floor. For Devon, we used light beige upholstery in the living room, a rush mat, and cane furniture, which blends in with the floor and creates a solid mass of light color that offsets the darkness of the wall.

Instead of the standard height coffee tables—usually twelve to fourteen inches—we used two twenty-seven-foot high tables in front of the sofa. Along with being more interesting than a low coffee table, these also cre-

ate an excellent serving area. As a rule of thumb: the taller the table, the smaller its top should be; the lower it is, the larger it can be.

Devon had his heart set on hanging a picture that was so large it would have meant eliminating the sofa if we were to hang it normally. The beam, which ran lengthwise across the ceiling near the wall, cut off the eighteen inches of height we needed, so we built blocks out to the width of the beam. This enabled us to hang the painting from the beam and almost from the ceiling.

Devon wanted a regular bed rather than a sofa bed so we had a frame made with an upholstered headboard and footboard. With pillows, it looks like another sofa. The windows are covered in bamboo blinds, which are very chic with either traditional or contemporary furnishings.

completely open mind about color. There's too much to choose from and you'll become confused. "Make a list of all the colors you like, then limit your list to your first three choices," advises Ronald Bricke. "Don't even consider any other colors on that trip. If you don't find what you want the first time, then select another three colors to shop for."

• Never pick out a color while you are in the shop. Color changes according to its surroundings. Even by the shop window, the direction or intensity of light is likely to be different than the light in your apartment. Always bring chips home so they can be viewed in the room where they will be used.

• Never make your decision by asking the salesman's opinion. He'll give it to the best of his ability—but if he were a decorator, he wouldn't be selling paint!

• Try the color in stages. When you're at the paint store, try to get at least six chips of a color that you are particularly interested in trying. Tape those together on a piece of paper and tape that paper to the wall. If you have other colors on hand—for example, a swatch of fabric—tape that up also. Anything that gives you an idea of what the color will be like when it's up on the wall will be helpful.

• Buy a small can of the color you plan to use and paint a largish section with it. "There's a radical difference between looking at a paint chip and seeing the whole room painted," Gerald Kuhn warns. "When you paint a section of the wall, you take the guesswork out of selecting a color. Either you'll love it or you'll paint over it."

If you've never painted the wall a color, it's natural to be wary. However, you can always paint over a color or ad-

just it between the first and second coats. Almost the only mistake you can make is not to try a color. Plain walls tend to be plain boring!

Using Paint Effectively

Is there really a difference between expensive and less expensive paints? When is an oil-based paint preferable to latex? Why should you spend more for good brushes and rollers? Just when you're ready to ask these questions, there are twelve people in line behind you and the salesman is in no mood to hold a seminar.

The special advantage of paint is that you can do a professional job yourself—when you know what to do. Following are painting tips provided by Neil Janovic, vice president of the New York–based paint chain, Janovic Plaza.

DECORATING DILEMMA

Color Adds Class

Jodi Deutsch met her husband, Alan, through her job as an art director for one of the major advertising agencies. He was the client and he liked her style. They took a one-bedroom apartment when they returned from their honeymoon. Alan wants to start his own business in the next few years, so they decided to keep their expenditures to a minimum.

"I'd like the apartment to be very chic," Jodi explained to their decorator. "We don't want to invest in expensive furniture, antiques, or fine paintings. That sort of thing will come later. For now we want a place that's interesting and memorable-looking."

Other than its river view, the apartment has no particular distinction. Jodi and Alan were willing to do any manual labor, such as painting or refinishing floors, themselves.

DESIGNER: GERALD KUHN

Jodi and Alan wanted the sizzle more than the steak. They were looking for showmanship to turn their rather ordinary apartment into a place with character. Almost the only way to do this inexpensively is with color used boldly.

A dramatic use of color doesn't necessarily mean you need a dramatic color. We used a medium shade of gray throughout. The color looks expensive and is easy to live with. In this particular instance, it served a double purpose: Jodi and Alan didn't want to spend a lot on their sofa, and the best thing that you can do with an inexpensive piece is to make it "disappear"—that is, to paint the wall the same color as the sofa so even the discerning eye won't notice whether or not you spent a fortune on fabric!

In the bedroom, we used a visual trick: the whole room is gray, including the curtains, the carpeting, and the bedcovering. The only slash of color is a large white circle that stands out in dramatic relief over the bed, creating the impression of a huge high-ceilinged dome.

In the living room, we created an extravagant looking painting with a wall-long screen, which folds out from behind the sofa. Alan made the screen by hinging plywood boards together and Jodi painted the screen in subtle bands of gray, gray-green, and green. Jodi painted freehand and the stripes aren't absolutely straight and some of the color ran. This effect is a more interesting treatment than definite razor-sharp lines.

The screen is thirty inches high, which is high enough to frame the sofa and low enough to leave the upper portion of the wall bare and uncluttered. This strong, low horizontal element draws the eye downward and makes the space above the screen seem bigger—which creates the illusion of higher ceilings.

The long wall opposite the sofa presented a problem. It called for a big picture or painting that could make a major statement. A small picture would be insignificant. Since they didn't want to invest in major artwork, we hung six framed photographs side by side. The frames are black and the matting is cream. Because the photographs were hung only 3/4″ apart, they appear at first glance to be one long picture—which is a more interesting presentation than six separate pictures. The pictures are hung slightly below the eye level of a person who is standing by the wall. Hanging pictures a bit lower than expected often calls more attention to artwork than when they are hanging at eye level.

The subtly-striped Berber rug is 8′ x 11′, which is large enough to accommodate all the furniture in the seating area.

The dining table is by the window. Jodi resisted this at first because it seemed inconvenient to bring food all the way across the living room from the kitchen. But after living with the layout for just a few days, she found this became her favorite place in the apartment. She finds it's much more pleasant to eat by the window where she can enjoy the view than at the back of the room.

The lighting here is both dramatic and practical. Uplights behind the screen create a soft romantic background light. A ceiling track lights the foyer, the wall of photographs and the dining area. Standing lamps for reading are on either side of the sofa.

Storage was a major problem for Jodi and Allen. They needed drawers, bookshelves, a place for the television, the stereo, clothing, and all of Jodi's magazines and notebooks. Three gray Formica units were placed next to each other in a pyramid, with a tall closed cabinet beside a chest of drawers one step lower. The chest of drawers is the lowest of the three units. It's sometimes more interesting to have three heights in bookshelves or chests than one monolithic block, which can look heavy and bulky in a small space.

It's often advisable to put two pieces of furniture next to each other so the furniture seems to fill less floorspace, as we did by placing the desk the long way next to the bed. It's a comfortable arrangement for Jodi because there is room for the breakfast tray without disturbing her papers, and the desk lamp can also serve as a reading lamp.

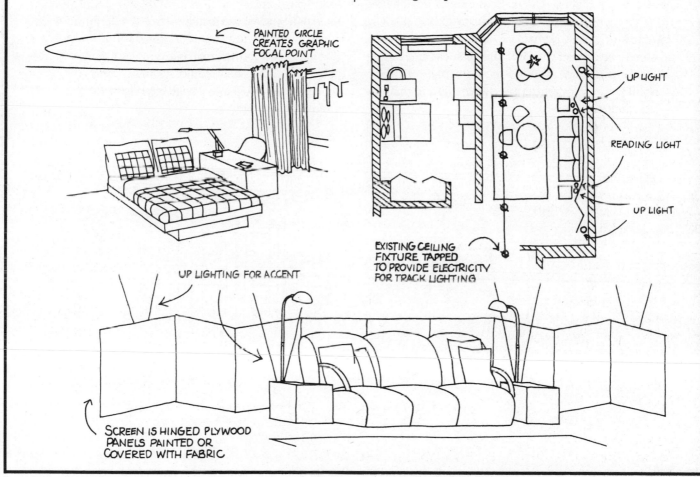

PAINTED CIRCLE CREATES GRAPHIC FOCAL POINT

UP LIGHT

READING LIGHT

UP LIGHT

EXISTING CEILING FIXTURE TAPPED TO PROVIDE ELECTRICITY FOR TRACK LIGHTING

UP LIGHTING FOR ACCENT

SCREEN IS HINGED PLYWOOD PANELS PAINTED OR COVERED WITH FABRIC

Using a Primer

A primer is necessary because it seals the surface and eliminates all porous spots on the wall. This means the top coat will adhere better and be more resistant to splitting or chipping. The chemical qualities in primers are catalysts for colorants, which means that the colors in your top coat will be much clearer and stronger than if the paint were applied directly to the wall.

You will get comparable results by applying primer with a brush, roller, or spray gun. Primers are available in oil- or water-based compounds. Oil-based primers are advisable for old buildings with paint-encrusted walls. Otherwise, use a latex. A latex primer is much easier to work with, you can clean up with soap and water, there's no smell, and it dries within an hour or two so you can do a top coat the same day.

DECORATING DILEMMA

Highlighting Art

Two years ago, Steve Denning opened his small avant garde gallery in Soho. His taste in painters, combined with the contacts he had made working uptown, brought him almost immediate prominence. He put all the money he earned back into the business and continued living in a small walk-up on the fringes of Greenwich Village. A few months ago, Steve realized that was a false economy.

"This is a very social business and it's important for a dealer to bring clients back to his apartment for a drink. I need a place that looks like I have money behind me. Nobody wants to buy from a hungry dealer," he explained to his decorator.

Steve planned the investment in his apartment the same way he selects art: always buy the best even if it's a small piece. His resources are still limited so he decided to take a studio in a fine midtown building rather than a bigger place in a less desirable area. Since Steve's main objective was to display artwork so temptingly that a client might want to buy a lithograph on impulse, it was important for the apartment to have gallery-quality perfection. The bed couldn't show, and the color scheme had to be a low-keyed, expensive-looking background for artwork.

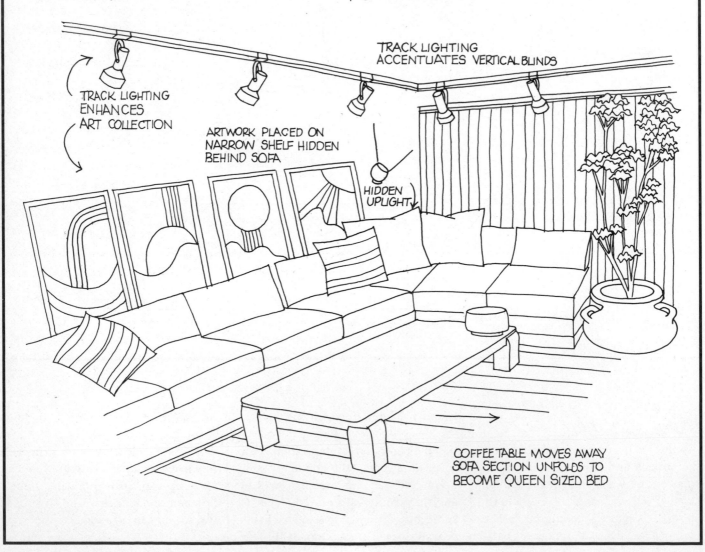

TRACK LIGHTING ACCENTUATES VERTICAL BLINDS

TRACK LIGHTING ENHANCES ART COLLECTION

ARTWORK PLACED ON NARROW SHELF HIDDEN BEHIND SOFA

HIDDEN UPLIGHT

COFFEE TABLE MOVES AWAY SOFA SECTION UNFOLDS TO BECOME QUEEN SIZED BED

DECORATING DILEMMA

The walls and floors of the apartment were in fine condition, but the kitchen was a relic. Steve doesn't cook often enough to care about replacing the cabinets or appliances. He wanted a cosmetic treatment for the kitchen that would bring the kitchen up to the same decorative caliber as the rest of the apartment.

DESIGNER: STANLEY HURA

Steve is a very knowledgeable client and very savvy about showmanship. Since the best way to show off artwork is against either very dark or very light walls, we chose a dark gray background. After the floors were stripped, they were finished with a gray-tinted high-gloss polyurethane.

The dark walls make the only expensive items in the apartment—the white modular sofa and the aluminum vertical blinds—stand out and seem doubly important. Since the purpose of the apartment is to show off art handsomely, we gave extra thought to displaying the pictures so they can be seen easily and be the focal point of the room. Our solution was to build a narrow ledge behind the sofa and prop the pictures on it. This way you can easily change the artwork—but more importantly, the pictures are at eye level when you're sitting and it is a comfortable way to view them.

Steve needed gallery-quality lighting to show off the pictures. This necessitated a four-sided track system so the lighting can always be turned to any place in the room he chooses to put a sculpture or a painting.

The modular sofa contains a folding queen-sized bed. Pillows are stored in a chest next to the sofa. The only other storage area in the room is a wall of bookshelves. The shelves are made of nine-inch-deep board from the lumberyard that Steve painted in a high-gloss black. The shelves store the stereo, the television, and his record collection. Extra papers and business records are stored on the shelf in straw baskets and black lacquer boxes.

The four black upholstered Parsons chairs at the dining table pick up the black accent from the shelves and can also serve as extra chairs around the sofa for parties.

In the kitchen, the ancient cabinets and appliances were painted with a glossy black urethane paint that has a lacquerlike finish. Steve did the painting himself and used the money he saved to buy black Pirelli flooring. Pirelli flooring is the embossed black rubber squares that you often see in industrial installations. It's available at most places that sell linoleum. A wallpaper with a gray background and subtle black-and-white-checked lines ties the decor of the kitchen into the color scheme of the rest of the apartment.

How Much Paint to Buy

Figure out the square footage of the wall and ceiling surface and subtract any windows, doors, or archways. (To obtain the square feet of a wall, multiply its height by its width. For a ceiling, multiply length by width.) Then figure that each gallon of paint will cover 400 square feet. If you've used a good primer, you'll get 10 to 20 percent more coverage on the first coat, and the second coat calls for 10 percent less paint than the first coat. (Unless you will be painting over exactly the same color, plan to use two coats.)

Look for Quality Paint

There are tremendous differences between good paints and cheap ones. A less expensive paint can cost you more in the long run because it doesn't go as far or cover as well. Although both types weigh a full gallon, there's a higher percentage of clay and fillers in an inexpensive paint, which is why a gallon may cover only 300 square feet, while a better paint will cover 400 to 500 square feet. There's also a difference in durability. Because better paints are denser and less porous, the colors will last longer and wash better.

Paint is a blind item and it's important that you buy at a store that is reliable. Most paint manufacturers make several grades of paint, so you can't buy by label alone. You need to be able to trust the store that's selling the paint.

Getting Your Color

Custom-blended colors are mixed at the paint store and are 10 to 40 percent more expensive than factory mixed paints. They are not necessarily worth the extra cost. The only time you should buy custom-mixed paint is when you can't find a comparable color in a pre-mixed paint. In the pastel shades, the quality of a custom-mixed paint is comparable to the factory blend. In the deeper shades, it's usually inferior because the factory can grind in the pigments better than any paint store can. As the colors get darker, the prices increase because more pigment is added to the paint.

You can create your own paint colors for considerably less than the cost of custom-mixed paints. Tints will give you great results in the pastel or mid-tone shades. Before you start, the store will show you a color band that indicates what shade you will get by using a quarter or half tube to a gallon of white paint. This takes the guesswork out of working with tints. You can also use the tints to adjust colors. If you have a color with too much pink, for example, you can neutralize it with a green tint.

Oil-Based versus Water-Based Paint

Professional painters often say it's necessary to use oil-based paints because they are used to oil and they are loath to change. There are relatively few advantages to an oil paint unless you live in a very old building where there is sometimes a powdery surface or where casein-based or very inexpensive paints have been used previously. The oil-based paint will penetrate and adhere better under these circumstances. But there are several disadvantages to oil: it doesn't maintain its color as well as latex paint, and it loses its gloss more quickly than latex.

Latex gives you better color retention. It's easier to apply, and for twenty-four hours you can do touch-ups that will blend in with the rest of the area. You can't do this with oil-based paint. Recently manufacturers have introduced an anti-spatter ingredient in the better latexes. Ask about this. Other advantages to latex are that it dries more quickly, there's less odor, and it's easier to clean yourself and your brushes.

Preparing Your Walls

Spackle, used for small cracks and nail holes or settling cracks, comes in powdered and ready-mixed forms. The ready-mixed is far easier to use and is recommended. Plaster is used for larger holes. Use patching plaster rather than plaster of Paris, because it dries more slowly and gives you more time to work.

When to Paint

If you are using an oil-based paint, you should never paint on a rainy day. Oil-based paints dry very slowly and the moisture will sometimes seep into the paint and leave foggy spots. It's always best to paint on a clear, dry day.

Paint Finishes

- A *flat finish* reflects the least amount of light and has a matte look. It shows the least defects on a surface, so is a good choice for masking flaws, but it is also the least washable.
- The *velvet* or *eggshell finish* is flat when you look at it straight on and has a slight sheen from the side. It's a good choice for darker colors because it is much more washable than a flat finish. It is particularly useful when you want to use one finish throughout instead of, say, a flat finish on the walls and a semi-gloss for woodwork. Until recently, velvet and eggshell finishes were available only in oil-based paints. They are now available in latex.
- A *satin finish* has a definite sheen, dries very hard and is quite washable. It is particularly good for woodwork, the kitchen, bathroom, or any area that's subject to a lot of touching or moisture.
- *Semi-gloss* has more sheen than satin finish, but otherwise has the same properties as a satin finish enamel. Your choice of which to use will depend on how much sheen you want.
- *High gloss* is the most washable finish. It has a porcelainlike sheen, which gives it the high-tech or wet look that decorators often favor.
- *Urethane* is a type of resin that dries extremely hard and is very, very durable. It stands up to abrasion very well and can be used on floors, furniture, kitchen counters, toys, or garden furniture. It comes in either a high-gloss or satin finish. The high-gloss urethanes have a very glossy lacquer look. Urethane paints should not be used on a stove top because of the heat.
- To paint the inside of a sink or bathtub, use a *two-part epoxy*, which comes in a variety of colors. It adheres chemically instead of air drying, so it dries very, very hard. If the surface it is applied to is perfectly clean, it will adhere beautifully. It generally takes three to four days to cure.

Applying Your Paint

Expensive brushes and rollers are definitely worth the investment.

There's a negligible difference in price between expensive and inexpensive equipment, but an enormous difference in results. You would probably have a better finish using a good applicator with inexpensive paint than a cheap applicator with good paint. The better roller will always apply the paint more smoothly, which makes the finished surface more resistant to peeling or chipping.

It's always advisable to buy an applicator that has been designed for a specific type of paint rather than an all-purpose applicator. For instance, with latex, a synthetic roller with a 100 percent polyester fiber is best. The same principle is true of brushes. In oil paint, a pure bristle brush will give you excellent results. But if a bristle brush is used with a latex, the brush will get soggy and leave streak marks.

Paint can be sprayed on, but spraying is an art. Painting with a brush or roller isn't. You have to keep moving with the sprayer; if you stop or don't keep up with the gun, you'll get drips or build-up. It's not a good technique for a novice to use.

Textures

Glazes are sheer-tinted paints that are meant to be used as a top coat. Decorators often use glazes to create unusual effects with colors and textures. For instance, a glaze of one color is applied over a painted wall of another color; then the glaze is textured with a sponge, bunched-up wax paper, or a dry bristle brush. This removes some of the glaze, which allows the undercolor to show through. The effect of the texturing and the two colors is very subtle and elegant.

Glazes are chemically treated so they stay wet longer and, when textured, are easier to remove than regular paints. You can't get the effect of a glaze by using two coats of regular paint. Glazing is usually done by professional painters, under the guidance of the decorator, who chooses the colors and the texture. However, an amateur can achieve excellent results. It's advisable, though, to experiment first with several colors and textures on a board before making your final choices.

You also can create very interesting finishes with sand paints or textured paints. For instance, stucco will give you a Mediterranean or Early American look, depending on how it is applied. These paints are also an excellent way to cover damaged walls.

With a textured paint, it is particularly important to prepare the walls very, very well. Scrape away all loose particles, sand any hard edges, and spackle to the best of your ability. Sand paints are very heavy, and if there isn't adequate adhesion the extra weight will cause chipping.

Although it is called "sand paint," it's actually a paint that has a silicate added to it. Under no condition should you add sand to your paint; it will simply sink to the bottom of the can. You can either buy a sand paint or buy a silicate additive to use in any normal paint. You can use as much or as little as you need, depending on the texture you want.

There are special rollers to give you different textures with sand paint.

WALLPAPER

If you're on a budget, wallpaper can be a luxury—but worth every penny. Buying wallpaper is not unlike purchasing a pair of expensive boots or a fur coat: definitely luxuries, but they make everything else you wear look expensive. Wallpaper has style. A yellow-and-white checked pattern in the kitchen, a nosegay pattern against a peach background in the dining room, or a smart maroon-and-white pinstripe in the hallway all create instant ambience.

Rules for first-time wallpaper users:

• Small-patterned wallpapers are almost always easier to live with and use as a background for pictures, furniture, and rugs than larger-patterned papers. "A rose that looked beautiful in a swatch will literally seem to grow on the wall," warns Kim Freeman.

• Never use wallpaper to cover a wall that is in poor condition. The paper will only accentuate the flaws. Walls must be perfectly smooth before they are papered.

• For ease of installation, you may want to consider a pre-pasted paper, although you should obtain permission from the landlord first. Another option is strippable wallpaper, which can be torn off easily. In damp areas (such as the bathroom) or in areas where the paper is more likely to become soiled (such as the kitchen or a child's room), you should consider using a vinyl-coated paper. Expect to pay more for these conveniences, however.

• To figure how much yardage you'll need for an entire room, measure the distance in feet around the room. Multiply this by the height of the walls. This will give you the total square footage. Deduct for openings (doors, windows, etc.) by multiplying their widths by their heights and then subtracting their footage from the total square footage of the room. Finally, divide the total area by 30 to see how many rolls of wallpaper you will need. There are actually 36 square feet per roll, but you must allow for waste and for matching repeats.

• The labor cost for installing wallpaper may be higher than the cost of the paper. In small spaces, you can install wallpaper yourself. Unless you are experienced, choose a paper with a

DECORATING DILEMMA

Clothe Your Walls in Style

William Brent has everything going for him. Five years out of Yale, he has already established himself as one of the gurus of high-technology stocks. He has a sixth sense for knowing when to get in a stock—and when to get out. Brent realized about a year ago that timing is equally important in one's own life.

"There's a time to leave the party," he explained reflectively to his designer. "I've seen too many young men get hooked on the perks of corporate life. I think I can make more money on my own—but even more important, I want to be on my own."

Brent comes from an old-money Long Island family. When he rented this studio apartment after college, his mother tried to foist off a load of family antiques on him. He accepted only the leather wing chair from the library. He is planning to use the apartment as an interim office while he looks for quarters for his new company.

Then he will buy a larger place for himself and keep this as a business apartment for out-of-town clients. Most of his clients are men and he was very specific in describing the look he wanted: "Masculine, efficient, and refined."

DESIGNER: LYNN LEVENBERG

Brent wanted the apartment to make an immediate statement for both clients and friends. This meant establishing a mood and color scheme that would be impressive from the moment one walked through the door. We did this with the wall coverings. All the walls are covered with navy melton cloth. This is men's suiting fabric and it's a very handsome color. We discussed the possibility of using felt on the walls instead, but Brent felt the walls should be "impeccable looking."

Brent lives in a modern building without any architectural distinction. There weren't even baseboards. The ceilings are the standard eight-foot height. This is normally not a situation where one would use dark colors. We made the scheme work here by installing pale pine moldings on the ceiling and floor to serve as a contrast to the navy, creating a crisp, fresh look. The pine

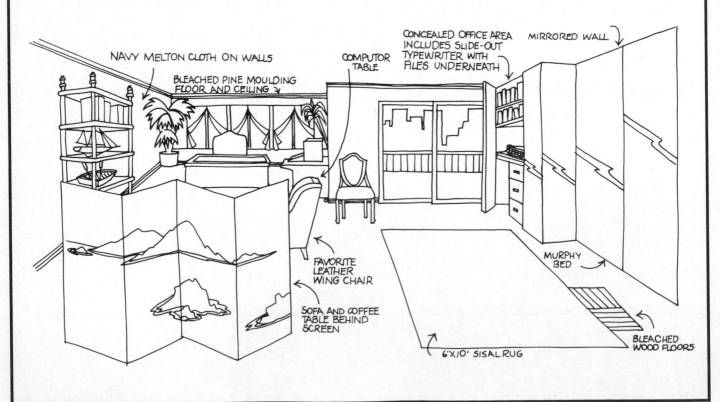

molding at the top of the wall draws the eye up and makes the ceiling seem higher. The pine molding at the floor was bleached the same color and matches the floors, which were stripped and refinished in the same light beige. (Pine moldings are available for less than $3 per foot at most lumberyards.) The armchairs and sofa are covered in beige canvas. Although both are substantial pieces of furniture, they appear smaller because they are on a floor of the same color.

The window treatment ties the whole scene together. Navy melton cloth panels lined with beige canvas were hung from a brass pole. They are pinned back to show the contrasting lining.

Brent didn't want his bed to be visible. Nor did he want a convertible sofa. Instead, we chose a Murphy bed with a mirrored cabinet and placed it between two storage units with matching mirrored fronts to create a complete mirrored wall, which adds elegance and glamour to the tailored navy and beige scheme—as well as making the alcove seem twice as large.

In the bathroom, we reversed the color scheme with a small-patterned beige-and-navy print wallpaper. The finishing touch: beige canvas shower curtains trimmed with navy ribbon. Brent's were shirred with a two-inch heading on a fat wooden pole, split in the center like a drapery and tied back on both sides with beige canvas tiebacks. They are lined in plastic. They could also have been on a metal rod with rings.

tiny overall pattern that doesn't have to be matched at the edges. Almost every shop that sells wallpaper has excellent instructional booklets. Installation takes more patience than experience.

FABRIC

Fabric-covered walls are a luxury, even for the very rich. Yet there are very few decorative effects that create such an immediately luxurious feeling as fabric-covered walls.

Although associated with traditional and romantic rooms, fabric-covered walls have recently become popular with designers working in the modern mode.

Selecting a Fabric

• Smaller patterns are easier to live with than overscaled patterns.

• Generally, patterned fabrics mix well if color families are similar and the scale of patterns is varied between small, medium, and large. If possible, select all of the fabrics you'll be using for walls, draperies, bed coverings, etc. before starting any part of the job.

• If fabric is to be applied flat to the wall, select a fabric with body, such as cotton, linen, felt, or men's suiting. If fabric is to be pleated or gathered onto a curtain rod, then the thinner the better.

• "Men's suiting looks great, but it can be pricey—from $12 to $26 per yard," says Lynn Levenberg. "But you can often find suiting off-price if you're buying out of season. Or you can achieve a very similar look by using felt in men's suiting colors—gray, navy, hunter green, charcoal. Felt is very easy to work with and it's a great buy. Seventy-two-inch widths are still less than $6 per yard. This means you can cover a wall with felt for about the same price as paint—and you'll have a really wonderful room when you're finished."

• The best buy in fabric, according to Stanley Hura, is sheets. And the best buys in sheets are in the single size. Usually two single sheets will cost less than one double, and you'll get more yardage.

Applying Fabric

Fabric is an excellent choice when the walls are in very poor condition. It is often less expensive to cover the walls than to repair them. Batting and furring strips (see illustration) become the buffer between the fabric and peeling or buckling walls. The furring strips frame the entire wall and hold the fabric and batting away from the surface. Batting is stapled to the furring strips and then the fabric is stapled over the batting. Double welting, cord, or ribbon is tacked over the staples to cover them.

Lynn Levenberg used a shortcut when she installed the fabric in her own living room: she simply stapled the fabric to the top and bottom of the walls. Levenberg seamed the fabric to-

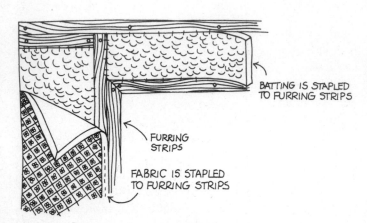

BATTING IS STAPLED TO FURRING STRIPS

FURRING STRIPS

FABRIC IS STAPLED TO FURRING STRIPS

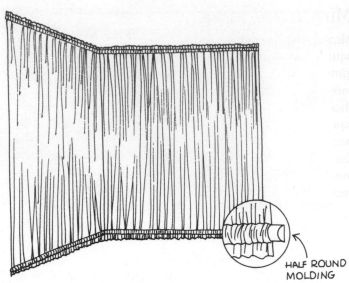

HALF ROUND MOLDING

gether before starting the installation. "I was lucky that my walls were strong enough to hold the staples. Some plaster will and some won't—but it's worth trying because it makes the job so much easier than applying furring strips. It's always richer-looking with a padding under the fabric, but it also takes three times as much work."

Lynn Levenberg also advises that you "use an electric staple gun when you're installing fabric. The job goes faster and you won't need as much stamina as with a manual stapler."

For particularly difficult walls where there is extensive peeling and unsightly roughness, a better approach is shirring the fabric onto curtain rods or half-round molding at the ceiling and baseboard (see illustration). Shirred walls create a very warm, intimate, elegant background for any room. However, the fact that you are in effect making curtains for the wall means you'll be using double the amount of yardage than you would for flat walls. Sheets are usually the least expensive way to do this.

OTHER WALL TREATMENTS

Carpet

Carpet can be an extremely effective wall treatment, although it may not be a good choice for a first apartment. For one example of making a decorative statement by using carpeting on walls, see the description of Richard Knapple's apartment on page 24.

Matchstick Blinds

Another innovative wall treatment is to use matchstick blinds. These blinds can be purchased in rolls and cut to fit; they are held in place by means of thin wood strips nailed to the wall.

Mirrored Walls

Mirroring can be appropriate for entire walls or just for portions. Either way it makes a dramatic decorative statement and adds glamour and a sense of spaciousness to your room.

True Mirrored Walls

Mirrored walls using large sheets of mirror are installed by glaziers. The mirroring can be installed so that it can be removed later; however, the walls will probably have to be replastered after the mirror has been removed. Clear ¼-inch mirroring costs about $7 per square foot; bronze- or gray-tinted mirror is approximately 45 percent more expensive. Add about $50 for each cut-out for electrical outlets. The price for mirroring a ceiling is about five times higher than for mirroring a wall.

Mirrored Squares

Mirrored squares cost about $1 per square foot and can achieve the same glittering elegance of expensively mirrored walls. In addition, you can install them yourself (see box). Mirrored squares are available with pre-pasted backs in 9″ and 12″ sizes. Although they can't be moved to your next apartment, they will dramatically enhance your present space.

HOW TO... Put Up Mirrored Squares

Mirrored squares are easy to install if you follow the directions carefully. Walls should be thoroughly cleaned before applying the squares. Check to make sure that floors and baseboards are straight by using a plumb line and carpenter's level (as in the procedure for pouncing, see page 20). Take your measurements carefully and be sure to allow for doors and windows. Mirrored squares can be cut with a special knife that you can buy at the same place you purchase your squares. The squares are difficult to move around once they are put up, so it's essential to be absolutely sure of your measurements before you start.

Using Closet Mirrors

Closet mirrors are a great dimestore buy at approximately $16 each. Use three or four wood-edged closet mirrors next to each other to create the effect of a mirrored wall.

DECORATING DILEMMA

East Meets West

When Kim Donovan completed her doctorate in fine arts, she was fortunate to land a job as an assistant curator for one of the major New York museums. Her job is to search out and assess the best in Oriental sculpture. Kim is admirably suited for this. Her father is an Irish-American naval officer who met Kim's mother when he was stationed in Japan. Kim grew up with the two cul-

tures and the two languages. Aesthetically, the strongest influence was the simplicity of Japanese design. It's reflected in the way she dresses—usually in plain black, which she accessorizes dramatically.

Kim's parents lent her the down payment for a one-bedroom apartment. After she bought it, she tore down the wall between the living room and bedroom. "I want space around me," she told her designer. Kim started collecting Buddhist statuary in Japan, which she wants to display along with her growing library of art books.

Kim believes that a well-designed New York studio apartment must be as precisely thought through as a Japanese style house. One of her favorite design elements, tatami mats—the traditional Japanese straw

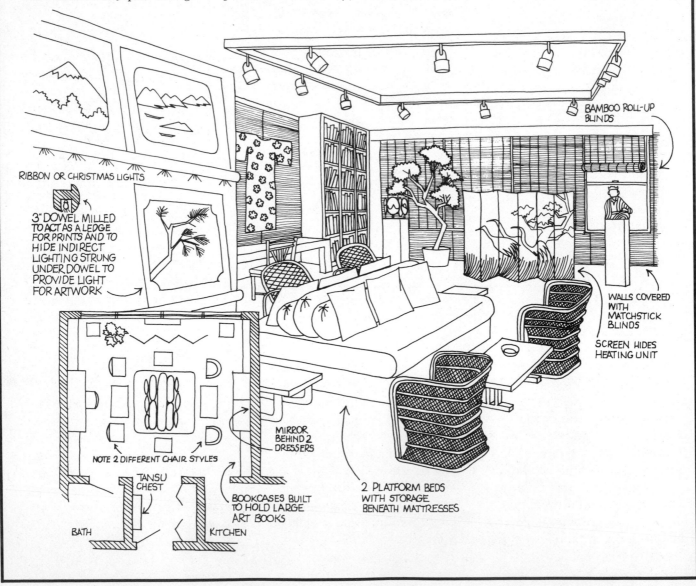

RIBBON OR CHRISTMAS LIGHTS

3" DOWEL MILLED TO ACT AS A LEDGE FOR PRINTS AND TO HIDE INDIRECT LIGHTING STRUNG UNDER DOWEL TO PROVIDE LIGHT FOR ARTWORK

BAMBOO ROLL-UP BLINDS

WALLS COVERED WITH MATCHSTICK BLINDS

SCREEN HIDES HEATING UNIT

NOTE 2 DIFFERENT CHAIR STYLES

MIRROR BEHIND 2 DRESSERS

TANSU CHEST

BATH

KITCHEN

BOOKCASES BUILT TO HOLD LARGE ART BOOKS

2 PLATFORM BEDS WITH STORAGE BENEATH MATTRESSES

mats bound in black cotton—was her choice for flooring. "I'd like everything to have a place, and the apartment to feel very serene."

DESIGNER: LYNN LEVENBERG

Kim was wearing a black turtleneck with black slacks when I met her. It would have been a plain outfit without the yards of hand-blocked batik wrapped around her waist obi-style. Clearly, she was a person who enjoys classic simplicity with dashes of decorative effects.

By eliminating the wall between the living room and bedroom, Kim had turned a rather ordinary one-bedroom apartment into a spacious, elegantly proportioned space. To immediately establish the eastern look that Kim wanted, we used matchstick blinds as wallcoverings. The effect is sophisticated, dramatic—and not very expensive. Matchstick blinds can be ordered almost any length from the eastern import shops.

The finishing touch for the walls was crown molding. Molding at the ceiling looks expensive, but it's available at lumberyards and is sold by the foot. We lacquered two-inch molding in a shiny black that contrasts handsomely with the shades and the ceiling.

A feeling of serenity is the key to the eastern look. We worked toward this by using a very simple color scheme, arranging the furniture very symmetrically, and using very few accessories. The subtle texture of the matchstick shades blends in with the cocoa matting wall-to-wall carpeting. We considered using tatami mats but decided they were too impractical. To complete the look, we replaced all the closet doors with shoji screens that slide on tracks.

One of the best ways to make a room seem larger is by pulling the furniture away from the wall, which is how we planned Kim's room. In the center of the living room are two platforms. Each platform is covered with cocoa matting, which gives it a built-in look. With mattresses on top, the platforms serve as a luxurious sleeping, seating, or lounging area. Each of the platforms can be opened for storage. The mattresses are wrapped with shiny black chintz quilts. Dozens of obi-patterned throw pillows become the focal point of the room. Inexpensive wicker chairs are on either side of the bed, and low tables that are used to display Kim's collection of jade and ivory bracelets make this area a complete room-within-a-room.

Kim is constantly adding to her collection of art books. These books are oversized and quite heavy. We needed sturdy shelving for them and built in floor-to-ceiling cube-style shelving that was painted in black high-gloss enamel. The shelving units were bought from a used office supply store and were painted in the same black as the bookshelves.

The long wall in the hallway becomes a gallery for prints. The prints are displayed on shelves that are lit with Ribbonlites ($16 per foot, plus about $50 for the transformer).

FABULOUS FLOORS

Floors may be the most underrated part of decorating. Many people worry about whether they need a new sofa or a better coffee table than whether their floor treatment is giving their apartment a finished look. That's a mistake. Next to the walls, the floors are the largest area of the apartment and will give you the most showmanship for your money.

There are four basic flooring treatments: carpeting, using area rugs, refinishing the floor, or changing its surface altogether by means of tile. How do you know which to use? What are the best buys? Which flooring will give the room the most warmth? The most serenity? The most sophistication? How do you choose a color? When is it best to use a pattern?

Here is how your decorators approach the selection of flooring.

CARPETING

Carpeting—which, unlike area rugs, goes from wall to wall—gives a room a finished, polished look. It can be the catalyst that completely changes the look of a room. It draws together the colors in the walls and furniture and unifies various colors into a scheme. For instance, beige walls and a maroon sofa suddenly become part of a scheme when used with a patterned carpet in those colors. Neutral beige walls and a beige sofa can go from nondescript to sophisticated when a matching or slightly darker shade or beige carpeting is added.

If you have excellent floors, there is no reason to cover them. If you're on a budget or will be moving soon, installing carpet may not make sense financially.

"Carpeting can be moved to another apartment if it hasn't been on the floor for too long," says Lynn Levenberg. "After a few years, though, the back-ing on the carpet dries out and will flake when lifted. If the carpet backing is okay but the carpet is not quite the right size, take it up and have it bound at the edges; then use it as an area rug. Carpeting that isn't installed should always have finished edges or it curls up and begins to unravel."

Plain or Patterned?

"As a general rule, carpeting should be in the same color family as the wall color," says Stanley Hura. "By unifying the two largest elements in the apartment, the room will seem larger. When walls and floors are different colors, a space seems more chopped up and smaller."

Every decorator has a private approach to creating a color scheme, but most agree with Richard Knapple, who feels that "the carpet should be the darkest color in the room because it anchors the rest of the colors."

$avvy $hopper

CARPETING

Carpeting is a major expense. Before you buy, shop in fine department stores and upscale carpet shops and note the colors, textures, and prices of the better carpets. Then shop the carpet "warehouses"—places that specialize in remnants or discontinued lines. You can often get the same carpet for half the price.

Most manmade fibers are in the $10 to $35 per square yard range, although some are as high as $45 per square yard. Wool carpeting is generally between $35 and $45 per square yard; special weaves might be as expensive as $100 per square yard. Many believe that manmade fibers are easier to clean but that wool has a better look. Both wear well, and ultimately your choice depends on color or texture rather than fiber.

To determine the yardage you'll need, divide the number of square feet by 9. For example, if the floor area to be covered is 10 feet wide and 9 feet long, that yields 90 square feet—or 10 square yards.

REMNANT CARPETING

Remnant carpeting is the piece left at the end of a roll, and is often available in the sale section at department stores or rug shops. Remnants are usually sold at about half price.

When you're shopping for remnant carpeting, you need to keep an open mind because you can't always find an exact color or finish. However, the price savings is considerable.

When buying carpeting that is to be used as a rug (not installed wall-to-wall), you can request sewn edges of a fringe finish. Most carpet showrooms have this service.

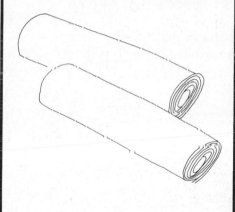

Designers quite often opt for patterned carpets. "Solid carpets are boring in comparison," says Lynn Levenberg. "Even a pin-dot pattern is more interesting than a plain rug. Patterned carpeting never shows the dirt as much as plain carpets do. Also, a patterned rug is a wonderful beginning for a color scheme. For instance, if you find a toast-colored carpet with a gray or blue pattern, you would have a choice of painting the walls gray or blue and looking for a tweed upholstery fabric that is a blend of the two colors."

Professionals often mix a patterned carpet with patterned wallpapers. This is tricky for someone without a lot of experience. "You occasionally see a room in which a large-scale rose-patterned rug is mixed with another floral pattern on the sofa and another on the wall," comments Stanley Hura. "This is a great look, but you must have a very discerning eye to carry it off. The easiest carpet patterns to work with are small-scaled repeats and low-keyed colors. You want the carpet to complete your scheme, not dominate it."

Decorators tend to be playful with carpeting. Although it's much safer to simply pick out a color that matches the wall, designers often create custom looks, even with standard carpeting, by means of borders. For instance, they might chooose a solid carpet and have a four-inch patterned border added that makes the carpeting as interesting as a rug. For that matter, they sometimes add several borders of varying width and colors. It takes courage to do this for the first time. If you are buying your carpeting at a department store, you can often get help from the decorating department in planning your design.

Industrial Carpeting

Carpeting is particularly effective with contemporary furniture. "It warms up the steel and glass and holds a color scheme together without becoming a busy element in the way a rug does," says Knapple.

There are fashion fads in carpeting just as in every area of design. In the fifties, shag carpets were popular; in the sixties, it was velvet finish (thick without any texture); in the seventies and eighties, the rage turned to industrial types of carpeting. The flat charcoal grays that were formerly reserved for factories and offices suddenly became popular in penthouses.

Fads either become classics or clichés—or both. And that's what's happened with industrial carpeting. Where it's appropriate, such as with black leather furniture, chrome coffee tables, light-colored walls, then it should be used.

"One of the major advantages of industrial-style carpet is that it has a flat finish and works very well in rooms where there are platforms or steps. It can also be wrapped around a simple box spring to give a built-in look," says Richard Knapple. "This is harder to do with thick carpets.

"The low-weave carpets tend to be a terrific buy and they also have a great look in contemporary interiors," Knapple continues. "However, we're no longer restricted to gray. There's now a wonderful range of colors."

Wool or Synthetic?

For years, synthetics were considered inferior to wool because they tended to have a sheen that made the colors seem harsh, and the finishes were often stiffer than those of natural fibers. This has changed. Now synthetics can be almost indistinguishable from wool—and, quite often, they have the best qualities of a manmade product in terms of durability, and the advantage of a natural product in terms of colors. Prices tend to reflect this change. Quite often, wool and synthetics are in the same price range. Your choice will be made mostly by eye and feel.

When buying a synthetic, be sure to take a sample into the daylight to check for sheen. Avoid synthetics that have a sheen—it's usually an indicator of a cheap rug and it will make everything in the room look less expensive.

Cocoa Matting

Cocoa matting has been very popular recently, for the very good reason that it has great style. It's a foil for English antiques and it also blends with contemporary furniture.

Matting's biggest drawback is that it can be difficult to clean. And it's not advisable for people with pets.

Before decorators started using matting, it was the homely stuff that covered diving boards. Part of its popularity was its relatively low price. However, the price of the matting is deceptive. Because the matting is difficult to stretch, installation tends to be pricey. Get the total cost before making a decision.

AREA RUGS

The principle advantage of area rugs is that they add color, interest, and pattern to a room. While carpeting will often make a space seem larger because it takes the eye out to the edge of the floor, area rugs can often make a space seem smaller. This isn't always a disadvantage. It can make a room seem warmer and more personal.

Area rugs are meant to do what their name implies: define areas. When a rug is too small, it doesn't have presence or serve a real purpose. Sometimes a small rug can be used under the coffee table as a spot of color. Be sure, though, its edges won't be caught under chairs that move.

In a dining area, the rug should always be two feet larger all around than the table. For instance, if your table is 4' by 6', then the rug should be 8' by 10'. You'll need this size so the chair legs don't get caught on the rug.

A 6' × 9' rug is a good standard size in front of the sofa. It's large enough for two club chairs to rest on it, and it's a size that you can almost always use whenever you move.

Larger rugs become handsome statements. A bigger rug will frame your furniture and have enough area to show off the pattern.

Rugs are a great starting point in establishing a color scheme. This is particularly true of Oriental rugs with their lovely low-key patterns. Generally there are three or four dominant colors in the motif, and almost any one of them will probably work as a wall color. If you use a variation of your rug color on the sofa and pick up another of the colors in a patterned side chair, you've got a color scheme!

A quality area rug is not only nice to live with, but can also be a good investment. Many experts believe that almost anything of value made by hand today will become tomorrow's collectible. The handmade kilims and Oriental rugs from India and China fall into this category—which makes some of them very good buys.

Kilims

Kilims are flat woven rugs from Turkey, Afghanistan, and the Middle East. "Kilims are still relatively inexpensive and they give you an opportunity to own a fine piece of art," says Gerald Kuhn. "They can be used in any room—even the bathroom—and with any style furniture."

"If your room is somewhat exotic, you can be playful with Kilims," suggests Richard Knapple. "They are flat enough so that two or three can be placed askew and look quite interesting."

Romanian Kilims are new kilims in charming folk patterns. They are one of the best buys in rugs—very well designed, reasonably sturdy, and very good looking.

Oriental Rugs

Oriental rugs have a two-thousand-year history. They may have been the original area rugs. They've been popular in every culture because their lovely, intricate patterns are a perfect background for every type of furniture. They are as elegant with contemporary teak as with Louis XIV.

Oriental rugs have been treasured throughout history as collectors' pieces. During the fifties and sixties they were out of style and it was quite easy to find a great buy. This seldom happens now. Most good Orientals, and even some not-so-good ones, are expensive. If you can afford the price, you'll be getting your money's worth. Older Oriental rugs, particularly those made with vegetable dyes, have been increasing rapidly in value. The best place to buy Oriental rugs is at an auction. However, you should only buy at a good auction house and you should always inspect the merchandise first.

"Antique Oriental rugs have soft colors. They are a beautiful background for any room," says Richard Knapple. "However, there are new Oriental rugs which have great style. One of the best buys is the new Oriental rugs from India, which have been bleached so the colors look as if they've been aged over time."

Until recently, all Oriental rugs were handmade—and expensive. Now, many are machine made and very affordable. A 9' × 12' new Oriental rug runs from $550 to $1500. When buying a new Oriental rug, avoid those with harsh, too-bright colors. They tend to dominate and overwhelm a room. In a room that is large enough, you might want to consider using two rather large rugs, either to define areas or simply to fill the space in a very lush way. That's the way rich Persians decorated their palaces centuries ago, and it's still a terrific look!

Dhurrie Rugs

Flat, woven rugs that generally come from Pakistan and India, Dhurries are often in lovely pastel patterns with pale beige, cream or light gray backgrounds. Dhurries were originally woven for Maharajas' summer palaces and used to be "decorator rugs," handmade to size and quite expensive. Now Dhurries are being imported in sufficient quantities to reduce the prices drastically—from about $350 to $750 each. The Dhurries in department stores today are almost the same quality and tend to be very good buys. Since they are light in color, you will want to consider whether it's wise to use them in a high traffic area.

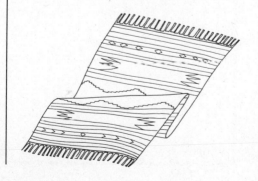

DECORATING DILEMMA

First: The Rug

Carol Andrews grew up rich. At twenty-six, she's learned how to handle money so it doesn't interfere with her life. "I don't think it's appropriate for me to live with antiques or with great luxury right now," she told her designer. None of her friends know that two libraries and a sports arena have been named after her father in their hometown. She would rather be known as a first-rate editor.

She started as a secretary and has now worked her way up to being a junior editor. Carol brings manuscripts home every night and reads every minute she has. "Books are the most important thing in my life," she says. The number-two item is exercising. She wanted an exercise mat and barre in the bedroom. "I hate standing in line for the shower at a club."

Carol envisioned a warm and inviting place. "I know 'cozy' is an overused word, but that's the way I want people to describe the apartment," she said. Carol had been sharing an apartment with roommates, so she had very little furniture to start with. Her mother offered to help furnish her new place but Carol turned down everything but an oriental rug and a lovely French-styled desk. The rug is real and very valuable; the desk is a reproduction but looks expensive.

The greatest asset in the apartment is the fireplace. Carol assumed that a sofa would be in front of the fireplace and the desk would be in the rear of the room. "I need a lot of light in here because I'll be working at the desk for more hours than I'll be sleeping in bed."

DESIGNER: RONALD BRICKE

Carol decided to accept the rug from her mother after she went into the stores and shopped around: she found so many copies of that style that she knew her friends would assume hers was a reproduction also. The pattern is strong and gives the whole room character. Carol's rug had a peach/melon background, and we picked that up by painting the walls throughout the whole apartment a clay color. Clay is a very warm and inviting color; it's extremely flattering to everyone and makes any space homey.

The upholstery on the sofa is a slightly grayish/clay and the tweed fabric on the arm chairs has green flecks. Yet when you look at them from a distance, both fabrics seem to match the wall color exactly.

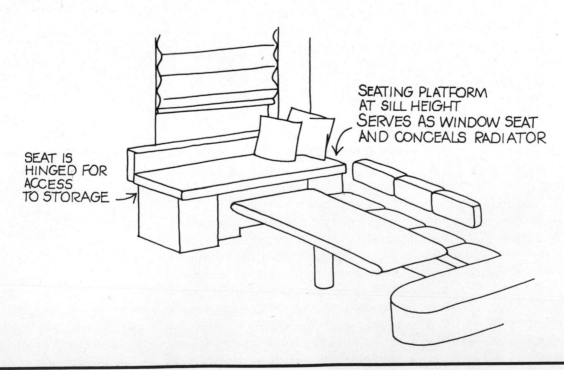

SEAT IS HINGED FOR ACCESS TO STORAGE →

SEATING PLATFORM AT SILL HEIGHT SERVES AS WINDOW SEAT AND CONCEALS RADIATOR

DECORATING DILEMMA

Carol's fireplace has a handsome mantle, and one's natural inclination is to put the major seating in front of it. Yet in this room that would mean dividing the space in two: the seating area in front of the fireplace and the desk area in the rear. It's never advisable to create two completely separate areas in a room. We used a swivel chair near the fireplace but placed the main seating in the middle of the room so it would blend in with the desk area.

The fireplace was wired for sconces. Carol had considered taking them out—"I hate those little phony candlelights"—but instead we used halogen sconces, which completely light up the room and do away with the need for track lighting.

Carol has been collecting pictures for years. Some are from home, some are from her travels, and others she found on Saturday shopping expeditions. The frames are all different and the subjects are also different. She wanted to hang as many as possible without creating havoc.

Groupings are easy to do. Get all of your pictures together and put them on the floor. Then you can move them around as much as you like before making any decisions. Different sizes and shapes are no problem. If you keep a straight line around the top and two sides, the pictures will seem to belong together. The bottom line doesn't have to be straight. Hang the smallest pictures nearest to where they will be seen. Over Carol's sofa, we hung the cameo paintings at eye level to the person who is sitting on the couch.

The biggest mistake with pictures is to hang them too high. Pictures should always have some connection with the furniture they are near. Ideally, the picture (or pictures) is perceived almost as one with the furniture.

For instance, the small painting by Carol's desk is hung much lower than one might have expected. But at this height it takes on an added importance by being perceived visually as part of the desk rather than being seen as a drop-sized picture in the middle of the wall.

Carol is a romantic. She has always dreamed of having a window seat where she can curl up during the day with manuscripts. High-rise apartments aren't really ideal for window seats, but we succeeded in creating a thoroughly modern one in the kitchen. A banquette was built around the table at seating height. On the third side—the window wall—the seating platform was raised to window level. With lots of pillows, it became a perfect window seat.

Although Carol's main focus is books, she must stay current with television because so many of her book contracts have subsidiary television rights. Rather than have a television and VCR in the living room and bedroom, we used a cart that holds that paraphernalia and can be rolled from room to room.

Carol's building is directly across from another high-rise. We installed sun screens in the bedroom that can be rolled up from the bottom so that Carol has both sunlight and privacy during her exercise session. A mirror by the exercise area reflects the light and makes the room seem much brighter. A wide dowel across the window wall serves as a workout barre.

TIP

"I believe that a rug should frame furniture. When a chair or sofa is half on and half off the rug, the area has a disorganized look."
—*Gerald Kuhn*

Sisal Rugs

"Sisal" is a general term for grass or jute mats. These are generally beige and usually handwoven. Sisal doesn't wear particularly well—it pulls apart, frays, and gets worn-looking after about a year—so sisal rugs aren't recommended for areas where there will be heavy traffic. However, they are a stylish solution for transitional apartments or for people who want to

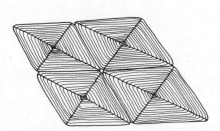

furnish a place quickly and inexpensively. There's a choice of patterns, but they all go well with either traditional or modern furniture. You can usually find a 9′ × 12′ sisal rug at Japanese import shops for about $100, which makes a sisal rug a real bargain in the short run.

Rag Rugs

Rag rugs are a wonderful buy. Some of the best color mixes are from Haiti. Use rag rugs with any style—Early American (of course!), contemporary, even English and Country French. They all look wonderful with the cheerful colors of this homespun look.

REFINISHING THE FLOORS

One of the sure signs that a decorator has designed an apartment is elegantly finished floors. Decorators tend to start from scratch—stripping the floors back to their original color so they can either be finished with a clear or tinted polyurethane, stained a very dark color, or "pickled."

The finishing color is determined by the rest of the decor. For instance, clear polyurethane over stripped floors is very sophisticated; it's quite near to the look of very old European castles, in which the floors are usually scrubbed pine. These floors are very effective with traditional as well as contemporary furniture and rugs. Light floors are particularly stylish in small apartments, where the rule is that the lighter the floor, the larger the space seems.

Sometimes a designer will take the opposite tack and refinish the floors in a near-ebony stain. This is the color floor that was often used in plantations where the very dark color on the floor made the white walls seem even more pristine. Dark colors *are* stunning, but

they are hard to keep clean. Bear in mind that the darker the finish, the more likely that dust and scratches will show.

Pickling

Between a very light natural look and a very dark stain, the most decorative and practical floor finish is "pickling." Pickled floors are sanded, stripped of their finish, and then refinished in a sheer color that allows the grain to show through. This sheer color is generally a very thinned down paint, which means that it's possible to match your wall and floor color. If this finish appeals to you, then you should work with a very fine paint store, one that is used to working with decorators. They will be able to advise you in selecting your paint and paint thinners.

With pickling, the floor can literally be a palette for creativity. Paint stores can mix any color you need for pickling. You can be as subtle or dramatic as you like. A blush pink floor blending into shell pink walls with white canvas and rattan furniture is just one beautiful look.

"Try bright red floors," suggests Ronald Bricke. "You can use a true clear red with almost any color wall—yellow, white, pale green, lavender. Or imagine an eggplant-colored floor with dusty blue walls and Early American furniture. You can also do patterns," says Bricke, who did his own living floor in a brown-and-white geometric (see page 19). "To do two or more colors, you must first start by stripping and sanding the whole floor. If you have parquet floors and want to use the squares to create your pattern, tape off the squares separately. You don't want the color to run onto the next square. If the squares aren't separated, or you're dealing with a slat

floor, then slash the wood with a razor so the color won't run. This is time-consuming—but you can definitely do this job yourself and have a very beautiful floor to show for your time.

"Sanding is the hardest part, but if the floor isn't sanded properly, you'll never get a smooth, shiny finish. Although you can rent sanding machines, most of us aren't very good at that part of the job. I'd suggest hiring a professional to make the floors very smooth and then doing the rest of the job yourself."

Bricke finished his patterned floor more than ten years ago, and guests are still commenting on it. "People notice the design and respond in a way they never would to carpeting."

Deck Paint

Deck paint is an extreme way of handling floors. It's very trendy and stylish looking—but it's advised only where floors are in fairly awful condition and you don't have anything to lose. If you leave the apartment, the paint will probably have to be removed. Deck paint is heavy-duty paint. It comes in high gloss and some very good colors. You also can have it custom mixed. The floor must be very clean before the deck paint is applied. It can be rolled on, and you will need two coats.

One of the advantages of deck paint is that it does give you a lot of decorating drama for the dollar. Many New York designers opt for sparkling white floors with pure white walls to create a pristine background in small spaces. For warmth and charm, two coats of deep red are a guarantee of a memorable room. Red looks particularly good with a small kilim area rug. In large spaces, your choices are limited only by your imagination. A very famous New York artist painted the floors of his 4,000-square-foot loft a deep marine blue as a contrast to the white art-covered walls. Even the plainest color, like battleship gray, looks smart when it's bordered in white or striped with sky blue or red.

FLOOR TILES

Some parts of the apartment, such as the kitchen, laundry room, or bathroom floor, call for a floor treatment that is different from that of the rest of the apartment.

One option is linoleum tiles. Many designs are available. You can buy li-

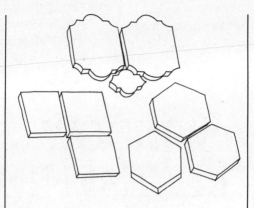

noleum tiles with self-adhesive backs which are relatively inexpensive and easy to install.

Pirelli floor tiles are embossed black rubber squares which can make a strong decorative statement.

Mexican ceramic floor tiles are available in different colors and shapes and can be relatively inexpensive—about $2.50 per square foot and up. However, having them installed can cost more than the tiles themselves.

Keep in mind that any hard surface will be noisy, since sounds will reverberate. Hard-surface tiling is recommended only for quiet apartments or small areas.

CHAPTER 7

WINDOW TREATMENTS

In decorating, there are some things you *must* do—like painting or refinishing the walls. There are some things you *should* do—like buying a pretty area rug. Then there are some things—like window treatments—that would be a real plus but that must remain a low priority until you've bought the essentials.

The problem with windows is that most window treatments are custom sized. This means waiting for the order, spending a lot, and leaving the window covering behind when you move. "Unless you're going to be in a place for a very long while, I wouldn't invest in expensive window treatments," says Richard Knapple. "If the apartment has venetian blinds, live with them until you've finished decorating."

In addition, most of us start with the most difficult windows in the world to make appealing—the standardized windows in high-rise apartments. Instead of beautiful woodwork, lovely moldings, and paned glass, our windows have convectors and air conditioning units. So what do you do when you're ready to begin your window treatments?

You take charge.

PROBLEMS PRESENTED BY WINDOWS

Convectors

The worst feature of most modern apartments may be the convector, which is usually referred to as the "radiator." It is usually plunked in the middle of the window wall, right in your line of vision every time you look outside. You'd like to cover it with curtains or block it off—but can you do that to a radiator?

You couldn't cover a *real* radiator with curtains or shelving, but you can hide a convector: it's not a real radiator.

"Convectors circulate warm air," Paul Shafer explains. "The misconception is that they *create* the heat instead of fanning it out. You can cover convectors with almost any material as long as you leave a slit at the top and bottom for the hot air."

In their office, Paul Shafer and Jean Weiner were faced with a typical problem: an off-center window and an unsightly convector. They solved the problem by unifying the styling of the entire wall. A plywood sheet covers the convector, and the top portion of the wall now appears to have two windows that are divided by small shelves. However, the "window" on the left is actually a storage area that's hidden behind venetian blinds.

Awkward Dimensions

"Most people accept the shape of the window as a given. That's wrong,"

Solving the Awkward Convector Problem

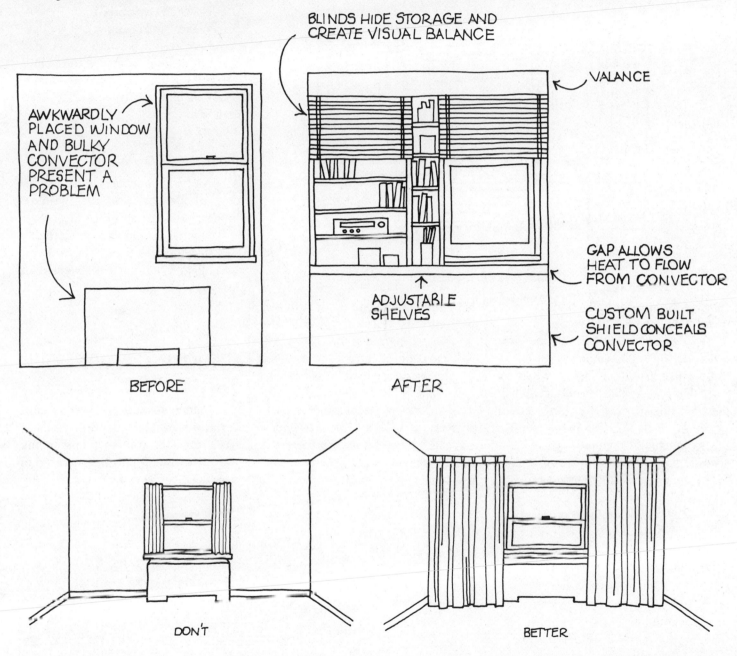

says Howard Kaplan. "The right window treatments can make your windows seem larger, smaller, higher, lower, or more centered. They can dramatically change the appearance of your room."

Here are some of the tricks decorators use to camouflage awkward window problems.

• *To make windows look higher*, create a valance that starts from the ceiling, or start the window treatment at the ceiling and continue it to the floor.

• *To make a window look wider*, start the treatment at the edges of the wall rather than at the edges of the windows. This will create the effect of extra window space.

Another way to make windows seem wider is to install Shoji screens that extend beyond the window. "They are expensive," warns Richard Knapple, "but very good-looking."

• *To make the window area more interesting*, "hang a thick bookshelf over the window and fill the shelf with pretty objects," suggests Howard Kaplan.

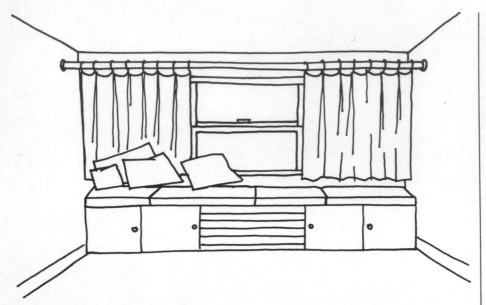

contemporary treatment, the bookshelves would be painted the same color as the walls and the window treatment would be mini-blinds in a matching shade installed at the ceiling (see below). In a traditional treatment, a valance and curtains would be used instead of blinds.

Mistakes to Avoid

"Always hang venetian blinds or window shades within the window frames," says Richard Knapple.

"Draperies shouldn't be more than a half inch off the floor," warns Lynn Levenberg. "Nothing looks worse than too-short draperies."

CHOOSING A WINDOW TREATMENT

Fortunately, some of the best window coverings are very inexpensive. Your basic decision will be whether you want the window covering to blend in with the decor or stand out from it. For

Below the shelf, install a thick brass or wooden pole for the curtains.

● *To make the window area more romantic,* install a window seat across the whole space (see above). What you are doing, essentially, is building a box around the convector. "Throw lots of pillows," adds Kim Freeman.

● *To make the window area more useful* "build in bookshelves or a storage area below the windows," suggests Jean Weiner.

● *To make the best use of the space in front of the window,* Howard Kap-

lan suggests building a platform sofa in front of it. "Most people don't use the five feet in front of the window unless they are checking the weather. That's a waste of valuable floor space."

Richard Knapple designed a window wall in which freestanding bookshelves on either side of the window serve as a frame for the window treatment, which could be either contemporary or traditional. In a

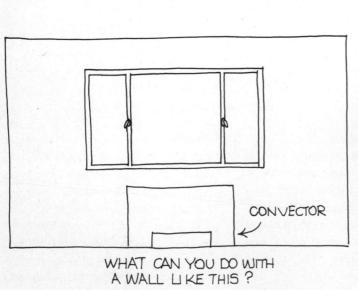

WHAT CAN YOU DO WITH A WALL LIKE THIS?

CONVECTOR

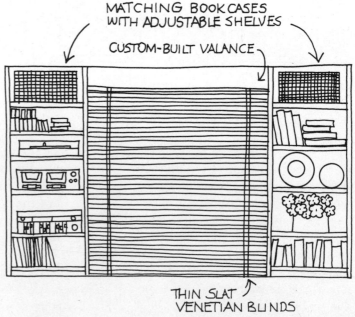

MATCHING BOOKCASES WITH ADJUSTABLE SHELVES

CUSTOM-BUILT VALANCE

THIN SLAT VENETIAN BLINDS

instance, narrow-slatted venetian blinds and vertical blinds are available in colors that match almost any paint or fabric. This means that you can have a window covering that will allow in light and yet isn't gorgeous, eye-catching, or interesting in the way that curtains or drapes might be. When you're not using a custom window covering, sometimes it's best to choose a style that will simply give the room a finished look and not call attention to itself. For other rooms, you may want the window covering to be interesting, even when it's not serving a real purpose—such as decorative shutters that don't block out the light.

Best Buys

- "*Mini-blinds* such as Levolors are the best buy in a high-styled window treatment," asserts Gerald Kuhn. "They come in a wide variety of colors. If you are lucky enough to have a standard-sized window, you can often buy ready-mades, which are much less expensive than custom." Narrow-style venetian blinds, measuring 36″ by 40″, are available for under $75—and now there's a special brush for cleaning between the slats!
- "*Vertical blinds* are always a solution when you need privacy and want a sleek look," says Kuhn. "When they are hung straight across the window wall, they create a very strong line important in a small space. (See page 46 for an example in which Kuhn used verticals as an integral part of the design of a studio apartment.) Verticals are ideal window coverings in a modern apartment. They allow you to have light, yet by angling them slightly you can prevent people from seeing into your apartment. For fabric vertical

blinds measuring 8′ by 8′, expect to pay approximately $100.
- *Paper Roman shades* are one of the newest inexpensive finds in the Japanese import shops. They filter the light and look crisp and elegant with traditional or modern furnishings.
- *Matchstick shades.* The general opinion among designers is "if you must, then okay." They're not a favorite because they look like what they are—an inexpensive window covering. Designers generally prefer *split bamboo shades* over matchsticks. The tortoise finish is quite attractive and blends in with any style furnishings.
- *Sheer whimsy*: toss muslin over a wooden dowel. Allow the muslin to crush to the floor on both sides so that it will look romantically full when it's billowing in the breeze. "The muslin costs less than $1 a yard—but it's a million-dollar look," says Kim Freeman.

Two Great Decorator Window Coverings

Roman shades are a classic decorator look. They can be made in almost any fabric, from inexpensive canvas to a lovely cotton paisley. The brass rings and pulleys are available in most fabric shops. The interesting pleated look is achieved by enclosing ⅜″ dowels in the seams.

Austrian shades are always a graceful window covering for a traditional room. The shades suggest the elegance of bygone eras with their voluminous shirring. Shirring tape is available in fabric shops. The best choice of fabric for Austrian shades are very lightweight sheers that will drape well. Austrian shades are beautiful on their own or as an undercurtain for draperies.

Roman Shades

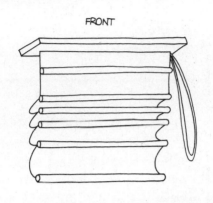

FRONT

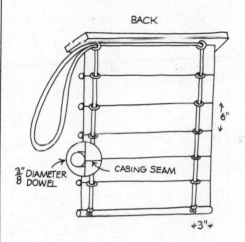

BACK

6″

⅜″ DIAMETER DOWEL

CASING SEAM

←3″→

The Real Truth About the Beautiful Curtains You See in the Magazines

One of the most beautiful looks in decorating is traditional draperies. They are full and lush-looking, and quite often so eye-catching they give the room its richness and character. Instinctively, we all feel that we could make those curtains—that it couldn't possibly be so difficult to find an inexpensive fabric and sew a hem. That's true. But there's much, much more to fine drapery treatments.

"What separates beautiful custom made curtains from the ho-hum variety isn't what you see, it's what you

DECORATING DILEMMA

"I Want a Romantic Setting."

Abby Jacobs is an unabashed romantic. At twenty-three, she's still young enough to dream of a Prince Charming. "I know it's old-fashioned to admit that marriage is the most important thing in a girl's life, but that's what I believe."

Although Abby is a dreamer, she's also a planner. "If I want a man to think of me romantically, I have to give myself the proper setting." Abby graduated from college two years ago and she's finally saved up enough to rent her own place. It's a small one-bedroom walk-up on the fourth floor of a brownstone.

"I've always yearned for a beautiful canopy bed," she told her designer. "And I'd like the living room to be as feminine and charming as the bedroom." Abby knew that it would be necessary for her to do all the sewing, painting, and manual labor. "I have plenty of time. Prince Charming hasn't come along yet!"

DESIGNER: STANLEY HURA

Abby was as determined as Scarlett O'Hara to have everything just right. We agreed that the least expensive way to achieve the look that she wanted was to use wicker furniture, with sheets as the fabric covering throughout. Her apartment would have been very costly

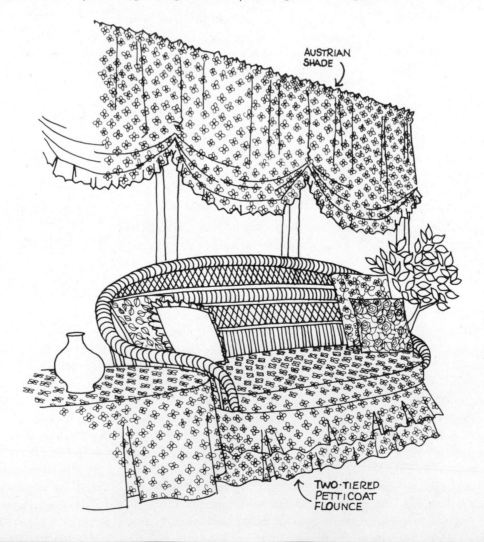

AUSTRIAN SHADE

TWO-TIERED PETTICOAT FLOUNCE

DECORATING DILEMMA

if she had had to hire an upholsterer, seamstress, or fabric hanger to make the cushion covers, window treatments, and bed canopy or to install the sheets on the wall. Abby's patience and persistence, however, allowed her to turn out a wonderful place on a shoestring budget.

The living room is a miniscule 12′ × 14′, and the Victorian-styled wicker pieces we chose are perfect for this small space. No one piece is particularly distinctive, but taken together, they become more interesting as part of a setting.

The sofa and the window treatment are the showpieces of the room. The sofa is extraordinarily pretty with a two-tiered petticoat flounce that matches the top dropcloth on the round side table and the pattern in the Austrian shades. It's a small-scale blue-and-white repeat, and we used the blue as our wall color. If you're

working with a lot of fabric and flounces in a room as small as this one, it's best to coordinate the colors so the space doesn't begin to look too busy.

Austrian shades are one of the most beautiful window treatments for a traditional room. When they are custom-made, they can be prohibitively expensive. However, you can make them for the cost of the materials—the sheeting fabric and the binding tapes (which are available at housewares or fabric shops). For about the same prices as ordinary window shades, Abby covered her seven feet of windows.

Abby debated whether to paint the walls or fabric them. Painting would have been easier and less expensive and she would still have had a beautiful room. But she decided that fabric-covered walls would look more luxurious and would be worth the extra effort.

Austrian Shades

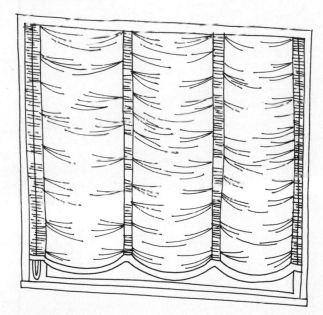

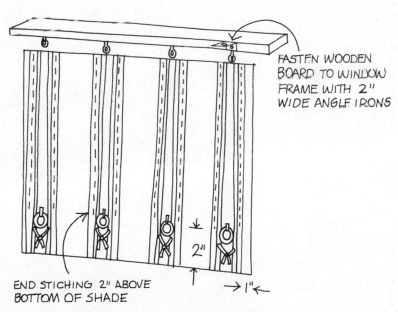

FASTEN WOODEN BOARD TO WINDOW FRAME WITH 2″ WIDE ANGLE IRONS

END STICHING 2″ ABOVE BOTTOM OF SHADE

2″

→ 1″ ←

don't see," says Lynn Levenberg. "Fine curtains are lined and interlined and maybe interlined again. The interlinings give the curtains their style. Without your realizing it, they add the appropriate stiffness so the bottom of the draperies literally seems to swirl onto the floor.

"When making curtains, you must use a full measure of fabric. In ready-mades, for instance, manufacturers normally allot fabric that's about one and a half times the width of the window, which is skimpy. Twice the width of the window is adequate. Two and a half to three times the width of the window is standard for fine custom curtains (sheer fabric needs more yardage). This can be a lot of yardage to buy when you add on the cost of the lining and the interlining.

"The finishing on traditional curtains is very important. They are almost always edged in ribbon, fringe, cord, or welting. The curtains can be hung on simple wooden dowels or more elaborately hung from under valances.

"Draperies should either hang a half inch off the floor or 'crush' to the floor. 'Crushed' draperies are very rich looking—but they are also dust catchers. It's a very luxurious look and only advisable in rooms big enough to accommodate the extra fabric. Hems should always be generous—at least six inches. This will make the draperies appear fuller at the bottom, and it will also allow you leeway in case they shrink in cleaning or if you need the extra length in another apartment."

Are beautiful curtains worth the expense? Yes, they definitely can be. And they are in the affordable range if you're lucky enough to know how to sew. All you really need to be able to do is make straight hems. You should look at expensive, well-made curtains and notice how thick they are, how they are hung, how they are finished.

CHAPTER 8

THE LIGHTING GUIDE

Lighting is the least understood of the decorating tools. It can make the difference between your place appearing cheerful or drab, romantic or cold, relaxing or off-putting. Designers know this—and that's why they always plan their lighting with the same care they lavish on the selection of color schemes and furniture styles.

"Your starting point should be to ask yourself what you need the lighting for," says Stanley Hura. "Is it for reading, for spotlighting art, for mood, drama, or simply to keep yourself from stumbling in the dark?"

Those questions may seem obvious. But how often have you seen an apartment loaded with tracklights that seemed designed to shine in your eyes wherever you look? Even with a dozen spotlights, you can still have trouble finding enough light to read by.

"You have to train yourself to look at lighting," says Jean Weiner. "Light is always around us but we don't always pay attention to it. When you're in an apartment or restaurant with a pleasing light quality, notice what kind of fixture it is, how it's hung, what kind of bulb it has, and then you'll know how to reproduce the effect."

Lighting is a strong element in an apartment. "Sometimes you don't need to divide a space physically— you can create the same effect with lighting," suggests Paul Shafer. "If you turn up the light in the dining area when you're ready to serve dinner, for instance, people will gravitate toward the table."

You should think of lighting as a tool of decorating and an inherent part of its style. For traditionalists, lighting fixtures are decorative accessories. They prefer lamps, sconces, ginger jars, or candlestick shapes to the high-tech look of track lighting. Usually the color of the lamp bases is in keeping with the decor, and the lamp shades soften the light. Typical of the traditional approach, the whole is more important than the individual parts, and lighting is meant to blend in with the background rather than become a focal point.

Contemporary design demands a different approach. Here, the colors are more neutral, there is less distraction, fewer pieces of furniture. Each piece must be important unto itself. Lighting is thus often used to focus attention on an object or create dramatic impact. For instance, against a neutral background, a spotlight on a vase with one single flower can be very effective. The light is used for drama and this very theatrical approach allows you to make a collection, a picture, or a rather mundane object seem important by its museum-elegant setting.

Whether your approach is traditional, contemporary, or somewhere in between, you should consider using lighting in a variety of ways—as mood lighting, reading light, background light, or spotlighting—for maximum flexibility in your apartment.

Here's what you need to know about the various forms of lighting in order to get the lighting look you want.

TRACK LIGHTING

Track lighting is a very direct way of getting light into every corner and onto every object. Think of how many lamps you would need in order to do this. When track lighting is used correctly, it gives a room overall illumination and mood lighting. Generally, you will need a table lamp, reading lamp or an uplight to supplement the track system.

Track lights should be used in one of two ways:

1) To spotlight an object. In this instance, you will select a "spotlight"—a bulb with a narrow focus.

2) To give overall illumination. This can be achieved by either bouncing the light off the wall or bouncing it off an object. ("Bouncing" means reflecting!) For this purpose, select floodlights—they have a wider focus.

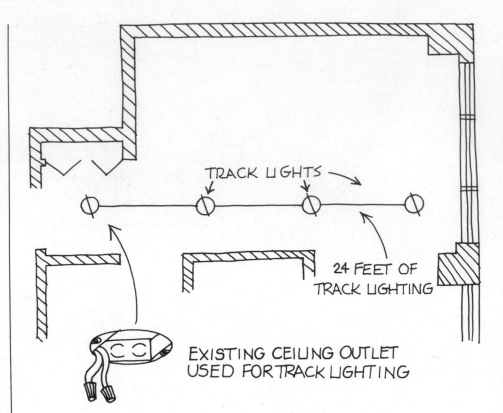

TRACK LIGHTS

24 FEET OF TRACK LIGHTING

EXISTING CEILING OUTLET USED FOR TRACK LIGHTING

best place to start the track so that it will light both the foyer and the living room. Installing a straight track isn't complicated; matching corners for

600 to 1000 watts, and a 1000-watt dimmer isn't expensive. Above 1000 watts, you generally need an electrician and new wiring."

Selecting Fixtures

When you are buying track lights, buy can lights that are in proportion to your room. "In a small room, use small fixtures and low-wattage bulbs so the lighting itself won't overwhelm the space," Gerald Kuhn suggests. "If you have a 600-watt track (tracks are labeled), then you have a choice of four 150-watt bulbs or six 100-watt bulbs or eight 75-watt bulbs. By having more small bulbs, the light will be diffused and softer; with fewer cans and bigger bulbs, the light will be more defined. Your choice of the fixture and the wattage should be made by thinking about what you want the light to do and whether too much light won't be overwhelming or too little light won't be uncomfortable."

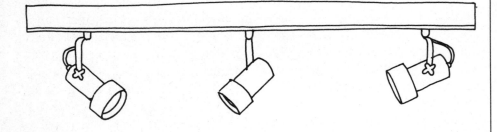

Installing Track Lighting

"Tracks can become expensive when they have to be installed by an electrician," Gerald Kuhn points out. However, an electrician is probably unnecessary if you are running a track straight from a ceiling outlet. Most apartments have a lighting source in the hallway, and this can often be the

turns can be difficult if you don't know about electricity.

"Tracks generally come in eight-foot sections, so it's best to plan on that module. In the apartment below, for example, twenty-four feet was installed by an amateur from the source in the ceiling of the hallway. That length of track will generally allow you

Avoiding Glare

One of the real nuisances with track lighting is the glare. This can usually be avoided. "By placing the track about three feet from the wall, you will be able to be very specific about where you want the light to shine," says Tim Meier. "You can also get a grid that will fit into the bottom of the can and deflect the light."

Gerald Kuhn, however, points at that, "With track lighting, it's sometimes more interesting to have the bulb showing. It's part of the tech look. This will mean that you don't have the additional expense of shields or a grid at the bottom."

"Lighting salesmen want to sell you their most expensive fixtures. And they are loathe to explain more than is necessary unless your questions are very specific," laments Paul Shafer.

Before you buy an expensive fixture, make the salesman explain its advantages. From a lighting viewpoint, there may not be any. Although decoratively one fixture may be better looking than another (and that's always worth something), the fixtures will give you equal amounts of light. The difference may be that with a more expensive fixture you will have more flexibility and be able to add specialized features. With the better systems, there's an infinite variety of finely designed cans that are especially designed for particular intensities. If you don't need fancy custom effects, then don't be tempted by the more expensive fixtures.

"The fixtures themselves come in an enormous variety of price range. The $10 fixture will be as reliable as the $100 fixture," says Gerald Kuhn. Three-foot sections of track with three cans are widely available for about $30.

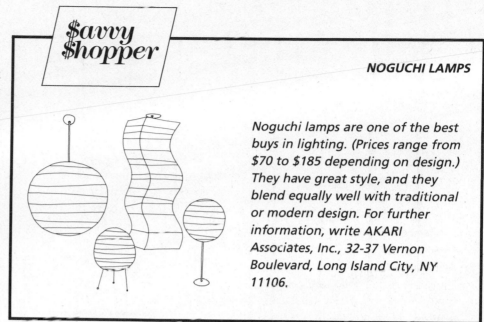

$avvy $hopper

NOGUCHI LAMPS

Noguchi lamps are one of the best buys in lighting. (Prices range from $70 to $185 depending on design.) They have great style, and they blend equally well with traditional or modern design. For further information, write AKARI Associates, Inc., 32-37 Vernon Boulevard, Long Island City, NY 11106.

LAMPS

Although track lighting offers a soft illumination that sometimes is referred to as a "wall wash," lamps are also needed to highlight specific areas.

Table Lamps

Some of the best looking table lamps are the least expensive. Well-designed porcelain lamp bases in good fashion colors with white or off-white pleated shades are available in 36″ heights for under $60. Stay away from psuodo-Oriental patterns or overly ornate copies of English rose patterns. The best buy is an uncomplicated shape in a good color. Be sure to use three-way bulbs in your table lamps so you can swing between ambient light and practical reading intensity.

"I like lamps to be smaller than you would expect," says Howard Kaplan. "The most important thing about a lamp is the light that it gives, and you get the same amount of light from a small lamp as a lamp five times the size.

"Small lamps don't make a major statement and throw so much light that your eye goes to them as soon as you walk into the room. Many people think that a big desk or writing table calls for a big lamp. I don't think that's right: the lamp is a decorative piece of pottery and it will make a statement just by being there."

Similarly, on a buffet or chest, Kaplan would use two small lamps rather than one big one. "This is a way of getting more lamps into the room and more sources of lighting, which is the way you create warmth. Two small lamps on a buffet four feet across are in perfect proportion, whereas one large one would make a major statement: Lamp on Buffet. That's unnecessary. The major statement is the buffet."

Standing Lamps

Avoid standing lamps unless there's a reason for one. The bases simply take up space and look gawky—except with a lamp that makes a sculptural statement unto itself. The only other time to consider a standing lamp is when you're using it primarily for uplight and you want a bulb that is nearer to the ceiling.

Hanging Lamps

There are many very chic hanging fixtures for over a dinner table, coffee table, or even side tables. Europeans tend to use more hanging fixtures than Americans, and the look is always very sophisticated. Over a large, low coffee table, a wide-bowl shaped green glass fixture makes a major statement. The cord is prominent and heavy, part of the look. Over a dinner table, consider some of the overscaled architectural cylinders and balls—sizes that at first seem too large until you realize how interesting unexpectedly sized hanging fixtures are.

"The ideal height for a hanging fixture is 5' above the floor," says Howard Kaplan. "This is high enough so the fixture won't interrupt table conversation and low enough to create an intimate atmosphere."

Kim Freeman adds that "anytime a fixture is hanging from the ceiling, a silver-coated bulb should be used to avoid glare."

A wide choice of styles and colors in hanging lamps is available between $15 and $40. Before buying, ask whether the price includes a canopy (the outlet cap) and the hardware necessary for installation.

Uplights

These are can lights, usually placed on the floor in the corners of the room to give a soft upward illumination. The extra light on the ceiling makes it seem higher, dreamier, and more interesting than if it were in shadow.

TIP

In the bedroom, swing-arm lamps mounted on the wall mean more space on your night tables. Buy the matching metal cord covers to hide the wires that run down to baseboard electrical outlets. These lamps are also charming on either side of a sofa, especially with fringed, shirred lampshades."

—Lynn Levenberg

Uplights are often used under plants, trees, or sculpture to project interesting shapes on the ceiling.

Halogen Lamps

The newest fashion in lighting is halogen lamps. These are fixtures that use a small, very powerful bulb that generates the equivalent of 750 watts of lighting from a 400-watt halogen "bulb." When the lighting is reflected off the ceiling, the reflective value almost doubles the wattage, and a room

TIP

In the foyer, replace the standard lighting fixture with an Oriental umbrella. These cost less than $10 and look quite beautiful with the light shining through the paper and spokes. To install, saw the handle off and attach umbrella with cup hooks to the ceiling."

—Lynn Levenberg

can be lit as brightly as if there were sunshine. These lamps can be expensive ($250 to $750), but for people with dark apartments—or those who simply feel the need for a powerful amount of light—quartz halogen lamps fill a true need.

"The only drawback with quartz halogen lighting is its slight bluish cast at its highest intensity," says Gerald Kuhn. "However, when it's dimmed, it mellows and there is still enough light to fill a space. For people who don't want track lighting, this can be an excellent alternative as a main lighting source."

High Intensity Lamps

Along with the columns of light and standing fixtures, there's recently been a surge in the popularity of high intensity lamps. These lamps are often very beautifully designed and they are small enough to be used in unexpected ways, such as being placed as an uplight on a table or as a spotlight for a painting.

CANDLES

One of the most underrated and underused lighting sources is candles. Yet candles are one of the lights most flattering to both people and rooms. Although we connect candlelight with traditional interiors, even the most old-fashioned brass candlesticks look quite beautiful in a contemporary setting.

"Candles are the best light for dining," says Kim Freeman. "Candlelight always make food look better and taste better than any lightbulb can."

Candlelight is always glamorous and gives any room a romantic look. Some traditionalists have gone back to the original candlelight fixtures, such as sconces and chandeliers.

DECORATING DILEMMA

"Help! I Hate This Dreary Apartment!"

Lilly Burt just returned from a wonderful year in Greece. She spent most of her time living on Hydra, where she was finishing the research for her fine arts thesis. "I love the quality of light on the islands," she recalls wistfully. "The sun gives everything a golden glow."

Lilly had hoped to find a penthouse where she could wake up with the sun in her eyes. The reality of Manhattan rents brought Lilly back to earth—below earth, actually. The most she could afford was a basement apartment with pipes in the ceiling and only two small windows high up on the wall. "It's more like a prison than an apartment," she moaned. "Is there any way in which this place can be made to feel sunny and cheerful?"

DESIGNERS: PAUL SHAFER AND JEAN WEINER

Although Lilly's apartment lacked glamour, she had a long-term lease at a very low rent. This made it worthwhile to install built-in closets, refinish the walls, and plan a lighting system that would enable her to live there without feeling claustrophobic.

We started with a typical basement with two little windows near the ceiling. Lilly wasn't exaggerating when she said it felt like a prison. With the realization that these windows could never bring in enough light to create the airy, cheerful place that Lilly yearned for, we worked from her dream rather than from her reality. Using laminated rice paper framed by plywood, we created a *faux* skylight. The rice paper appears as milk glass, and the plywood frame is installed at the same angle as a real skylight. It's almost impossible to know that there are light bulbs shining through the milky white rice paper rather than sunlight.

(Note: Laminated rice paper is $50 for a 3′ × 8′ size and it's available wherever shoji screens are sold.)

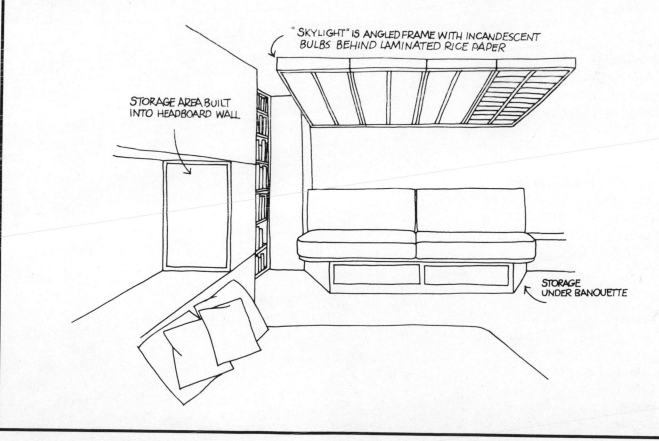

"SKYLIGHT" IS ANGLED FRAME WITH INCANDESCENT BULBS BEHIND LAMINATED RICE PAPER

STORAGE AREA BUILT INTO HEADBOARD WALL

STORAGE UNDER BANQUETTE

TIP

The most flattering lights are pink frosted lightbulbs. They can be used in any lamp and nobody will notice—but everyone will look better. Fluorescent lights give off the least attractive light. It would be best to replace fluorescents in the kitchen and bathroom with inexpensive incandescent lighting fixtures. If this is too much trouble, then at least use the full spectrum Vita-Lites, which give a warmer light."

—Lynn Levenberg

"Sconces died in this century due to electricity," says Howard Kaplan. "It was too difficult or expensive to wire them into the walls and so nobody bothered with them. But sconces that hold candles are wonderful—they decorate the wall and light the room beautifully for parties."

Many elegant reproduction eighteenth- and nineteenth-century wrought iron candle chandeliers are also available. "They can be hung from a hook over the table," says Kaplan. In Provence, flowers or seasonal wreaths are oven intertwined into the fixture.

CHRISTMAS LIGHTS

Surprise! Christmas lights are useful all year 'round.

TIP

Fluorescents or can lights can be used behind louvered shades to create the impression of sunlight coming in. This will make even the darkest apartment appear lighter."

—Stanley Hura

Christmas lights laced through a tree give a glittery, very decorative look. They also serve as mood lighting. Another tip: tack Christmas lights to the back of a shelf for soft backlighting of art.

CHAPTER 9

STRETCH YOUR STORAGE SPACE

The biggest challenge in decorating often isn't style, it's the practical problem of storage space. There's no way to have a handsome-looking room when there are shoes all over the floor, clothes falling out of the closets, and messy table tops. We all know this subconsciously, but it's not until we redecorate or move that the problem becomes acute.

Modern apartments aren't really built for modern lives. We all need clothes for the office, clothes for the evenings, clothes for weekends and special occasions. We have more books than we know what to do with, and every time we take up a new interest—whether it's skiing or playing the guitar—we buy new equipment that needs to be put away.

Yet even the most expensive places rarely have more than two or three closets—barely enough to hold out-of-season clothes and last year's hobbies. Where do you start?

Cruel as it may sound, the first step is editing your possessions. How ruthless you can be will depend on your personality. Some people can coolly look at clothing they haven't worn for three years and give it to the Salvation Army; others would feel bereft without their cheerleading sweater from high school. We bring our personality quirks to everything we do—including deciding what to keep and what to throw away!

If you have more possessions than can ever comfortably fit into your closets or the apartment, there is an alternative to disposing of them: renting a mini-storage room. Mini-storage rooms are in warehouses which rent small spaces for a minimal fee (approximately $25 per month for a 10' wide room).

Mini-storage rooms are a particularly attractive alternative for keeping furniture or bulky items that you might want in the future. This is the place to keep the piano your last lover left behind or the almost-antique chair you hate to part with.

When you're at the point of knowing what you want to keep, then you can begin to make a storage plan. This will call for creative thinking on your part. It means looking at every wall, shelf, door, and even the ceiling as a potential storage area.

CLOSETS

Your closets are the starting point in developing a storage plan. Determine your priorities. How much space will you need for coats, dresses, jackets, slacks, shirts, shoes and boots? Do an actual count. You need to know how much space you'll need and how many hangers will serve your purpose. Remember that the short items will be double hung.

To really increase your closet stor-

DECORATING DILEMMA

"I Feel Trapped."

Lorraine Blessing's apartment was ruining her life. She rented a studio apartment as a temporary measure twenty-five years ago and never quite got around to moving out. The low rent became even more of a bargain over the years. She felt trapped in a space that was too small for her. Her clothes were falling out of the closet, her shoes and handbags were being shoved into shapelessness, and the collection of dolls from her travels was collecting dust in boxes. There wasn't enough room to display them.

She might have spent years wondering whether to move, but she received a freelance assignment that forced her into making a decision. Lorraine is a secretary for a major corporation and she had an opportunity to moonlight on a project that would substantially increase her income. But she needed to work at home and she needed workspace. It was immediately apparent that she couldn't work in the confusion of her apartment. Papers were lost; files were being misplaced; the stationary for her assignment got crumpled under a dictionary that fell off a shelf.

"I am constantly tripping over things. No matter how neat I try to be, the place is never clean or organized. It's depressing. I'm embarrassed to have friends in. But I don't want to take on a high rent. I feel as though I'm trapped here with my belongings."

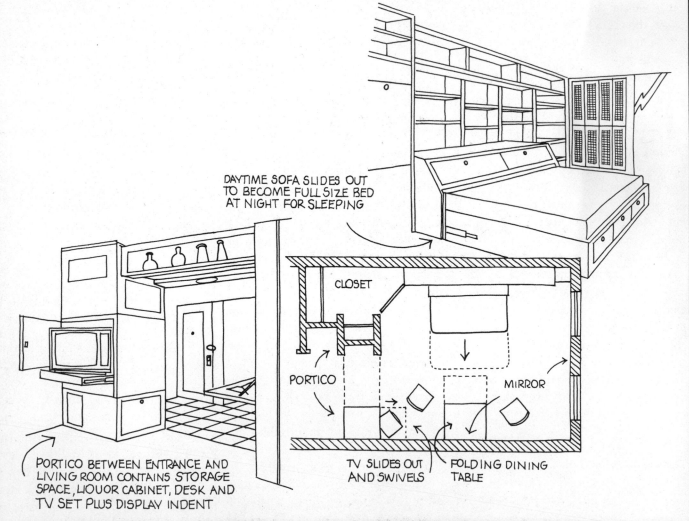

DAYTIME SOFA SLIDES OUT TO BECOME FULL SIZE BED AT NIGHT FOR SLEEPING

CLOSET

PORTICO

MIRROR

PORTICO BETWEEN ENTRANCE AND LIVING ROOM CONTAINS STORAGE SPACE, LIQUOR CABINET, DESK AND TV SET PLUS DISPLAY INDENT

TV SLIDES OUT AND SWIVELS

FOLDING DINING TABLE

DESIGNERS: PAUL SHAFER AND JEAN WEINER

Lorraine's basic problem was storage—or the lack of it. Her apartment is small by any standards, but there were many unused corners and areas that could be turned into closets, drawer space, and display areas.

When we first met Lorraine, her television was on the floor, her stereo was on the coffee table with books and papers on the dust cover, and her handbags were shoved so far back in the closet that it was easier to use one purse all the time than to stand on a chair to find another handbag. It was almost impossible to find anything. Clearly, Lorraine had outgrown the one small closet in her apartment.

We started by redesigning the closet. Her closet was in the corner of the apartment. We removed the doors from the closet and built in new doors at a 45° angle. This gave her additional wall space for storage behind the new doors—and *on* the new doors—without using any additional living space.

Lorraine's entrance hall and living room were one large space, and not very interesting in itself. We created a portico between the living room and hallway that divides the space in an interesting way, creates a dramatic entrance into the living room, is a source of soft overhead lighting, and, most important, gives an enormous amount of storage space. Each of the "columns" in the portico is a storage unit. There is now a special place for her television (which slides out on a swivel base) and the stereo equipment, as well as a door that drops open to become a bar—and best of all a special drawer for her handbags!

Although Lorraine's apartment was small, there were several unused areas that could be converted to storage. For instance, in the hallway there was a small space between two doors that had been used only for a light switch. We built a shoe storage area into this space. The shelves are at an angle so they can accommodate the shoes. In the space over the door leading to the bathroom, we built in an overhead closet for storing suitcases and out-of-season clothes.

---

age space, you'll probably have to redesign your closet and use one of several closet "systems." It's not enough to take your clothes out and rehang them neatly. The problem isn't that you're not neat, it is that too many clothes will always crush against each other and leave you with wrinkled clothing.

One approach is to build in dividers for the longer clothes and then double hang the shorter items. This can be expensive; it's also permanent. Better to invest in one of the plastic-coated wire-grid closet systems that comes with its own hangers. These systems may seem expensive at the outset, but they are a lifetime investment. You can move them or redesign them for any future apartment.

One of the best systems is Stay-neat, which is a component system of modular blocks that are screwed into the wall. Rubber-encased hangers fit into the blocks. The hangers are especially sized for dresses, slacks, skirts, etc. You can use as many blocks as you need and construct the system to your specification. (For a mail order catalogue: Stay-neat Closet Interiors, 132 Division St., P.O. Box 220, Dept. F, Boonton, N.J. 07005.)

In older apartments, it's easy enough to hang shoe bags on the door, but in modern apartments with bi-fold doors, you may need to create a space for your shoes, such as a narrow bookshelf against the side of the closet. Some of the shelves could be used for purses, shirts, or socks.

There is generally enough space under the clothes for a three-shelf bookcase unit. This could triple the amount of shoe storage.

If there is enough space for two shelves over the rods, then the top shelf can be used for dead storage (out-of-season clothing, suitcases, etc.). When taking measurements, be sure to note whether the top shelf is higher than the door opening. If it is, the shelf will have to be recessed at least ten inches so you can reach into it over the lower shelf.

Even when we start with the best of intentions, closet shelves usually become messy heaps of sweaters, hats, and shirts. The best way to avoid this is by organizing the lower shelf with divider units. Stay-neat and many other companies have plastic or steel di-

DECORATING DILEMMA

Making Space for a Relationship

Jennie Moran has a problem. She has a beautifully furnished apartment that she's crazy about. She's also crazy about a man she's been dating for the past year, Jeffrey Martin. They've talked about living together, but Jennie doesn't want to give up her apartment. Jeffrey is willing to move into her place, but there's not enough storage space for both of them.

"There comes a time in a relationship when you have to go forward or the relationship dries up," says Jennie. "I've held back because I'm afraid to give up my apartment. But I know I'll have to make a decision soon."

DESIGNER: STANLEY HURA

Neither Jennie nor Jeffrey have an extraordinary amount of clothing, but each needed the equivalent of one double closet and enough drawer space so they wouldn't feel cramped. Jennie's living room was already completely decorated so there was no way to introduce extra storage units there; storage had to be added in the bedroom.

The additional drawer space was easily arranged by means of eight three-drawer white Formica chests. Placed back-to-back and stacked double height, the chests created a dressing area. A mirror at the end of the chests was helpful for dressing and also gave a visual panache to the room. Across one wall, we built in floor-to-ceiling bookshelves to hold their extra books. No other furniture was necessary.

Jennie kept the closet in the bedroom and bought a system that enabled her to hang her clothes in a double tier. Jeffrey used the closet in the foyer.

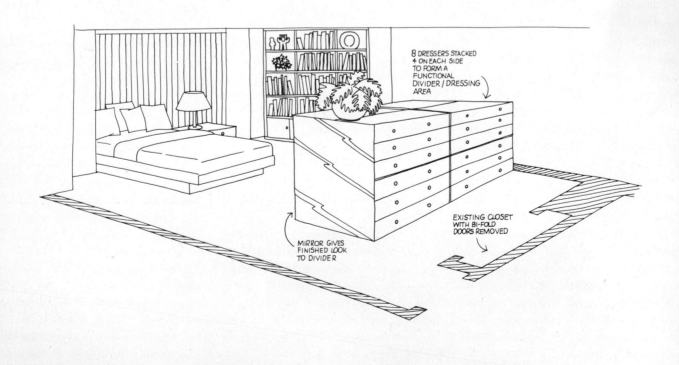

8 DRESSERS STACKED 4 ON EACH SIDE TO FORM A FUNCTIONAL DIVIDER / DRESSING AREA

MIRROR GIVES FINISHED LOOK TO DIVIDER

EXISTING CLOSET WITH BI-FOLD DOORS REMOVED

viders that clip onto the shelves. For small items, such as socks, stockings, or lingerie, you may want to use plastic boxes. The boxes will keep the items clean and may free up some of your dresser space.

You might want to use a wire grid system with hooks on one side of the closet to hold the things you don't want to bother putting on hangers. Housewares and hardware stores also have a wide range of closet hooks that will hold belts, hats, or a shirt that you want to wear tomorrow.

If storage is a serious priority, then you might want to consider building in extra closets. This can be expensive, but it's worth the investment if it means that you will be able to live comfortably in your apartment.

BOOKSHELVES

Whether or not you have a huge collection of books, every apartment needs bookshelves. Here are some creative uses of bookshelves to maximize storage space in even the tiniest apartment.

• The most logical place to put book cases may seem to be against the wall. But you can often use bookcases as room dividers and give yourself an extra six feet of floor-to-ceiling space against the wall.

• If you are using a bookcase as a room divider, decide whether you want it open or closed at the back. If it's closed, it blocks the view. An open divider tends to be more decorative. Along with books and heavy items, mix in small baskets or a little plant that will give the shelves an open, uncrowded feeling.

• Before you buy a bookcase, determine whether you will be using the shelves for books, files, or display. This will help you determine what height

$avvy $hopper

BAKERS' RACKS

The original bakers' racks were an integral and charming part of French patisseries. Although there is a difference between new and old wood, there is no visual difference between new and old metal— which means the reproduction has the same stylish lines as the original. Bakers' racks can be used as bookshelves, room dividers, and for almost any type of bulky storage. Bakers' racks are priced anywhere from $300 on up.

MOLDING STRIPS

Designers use molding strips as chair railings, to edge plain wooden bookshelves, or as a decorative element at the ceiling. These strips are available at the lumberyard in widths from ½" to 3" and they are often elaborately carved. They cost from 75¢ to $3.75 per foot.

and depth the shelves should be. If you will be storing mostly paperbacks, for example, then nine inches deep might be adequate: for art books, you'd need at least twelve inches.

• The least expensive shelving is often braces with brackets that hold the shelves. The shelves can be painted or finished in a wood tone.

• As a decorative touch, you may want to edge your bookshelves with molding strips from the lumber yard. For 75 cents a foot, you can give ordinary shelves a very finished look.

• Although you can use ordinary three-quarters-inch or one-inch boards for the bookshelves, and mount them with L brackets, the most elegant shelves are one and a half inches thick and are best constructed by a carpenter or a person who is a very neat workman.

BOOKCASE SHELVES CAN BE BUILT QUICKLY IF LUMBER IS CUT AND NOTCHED ACCURATELY

• Warning: "Shelves need support for every thirty inches of length. If you use longer shelves without supports, they will begin to sag in the middle," says Gerald Kuhn. See the illustration below for one way to support your shelves.

• When building in bookshelves, take advantage of any corner angles or structural beams that can help support a shelf or a whole bookcase. "Pillars next to the windows often create a natural indentation for bookshelves," says Tim Meier. "By building the bookshelves across the wall to the same depth as the pillar, the shelves will have a built-in look."

• "A whole wall of books might seem too dense and heavy for a small apartment," says Gerald Kuhn. "It might be wiser to do a complete wall of low shelves. This will give you a tremendous amount of storage space and yet the top of the walls will be left open and the apartment won't feel crowded. You also have the advantage of being able to lean a picture or put plants or objects on the top surface."

• A wall of cube bookshelves can have a very strong graphic look. This style also provides sturdy support for the weight of hardback books.

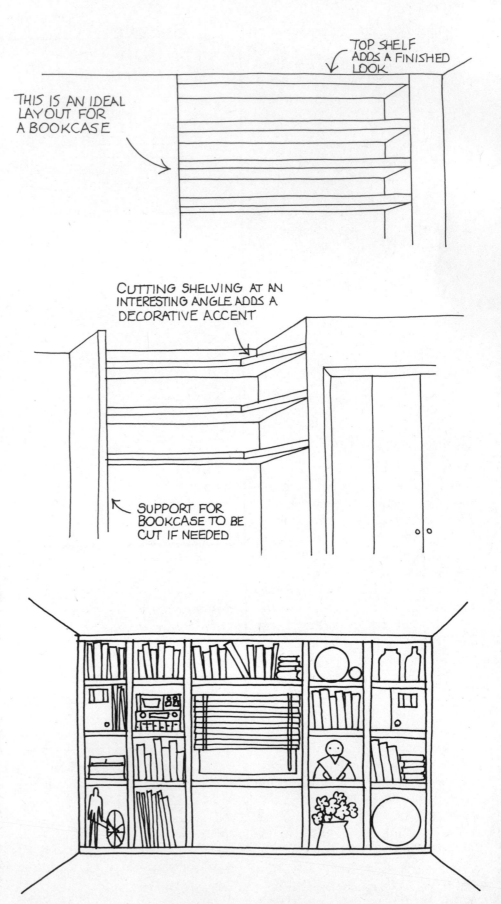

THIS IS AN IDEAL LAYOUT FOR A BOOKCASE

TOP SHELF ADDS A FINISHED LOOK

CUTTING SHELVING AT AN INTERESTING ANGLE ADDS A DECORATIVE ACCENT

SUPPORT FOR BOOKCASE TO BE CUT IF NEEDED

• "Instead of three bookshelves or storage units together at a uniform height and depth, it's often more interesting to use the pyramiding principle," says Gerald Kuhn. That is when a tall unit, a medium-sized one, and a smaller one are banked next to each other step-style. All the units should be in a similar finish, but they can each serve a different function. For instance, you might want a tall wardrobe, a medium-sized bookshelf, and a low chest of drawers. They could all be the same depth or pyramided in thickness. It's small details like this which give ordinary storage units a custom look.

• "Just as it's sometimes wise to leave space above bookshelves, you can also leave space below the shelves. By using one, two, or three shelves that are above eye level, you create an interesting focal point for the room and yet maintain a large expanse of unfilled wall."

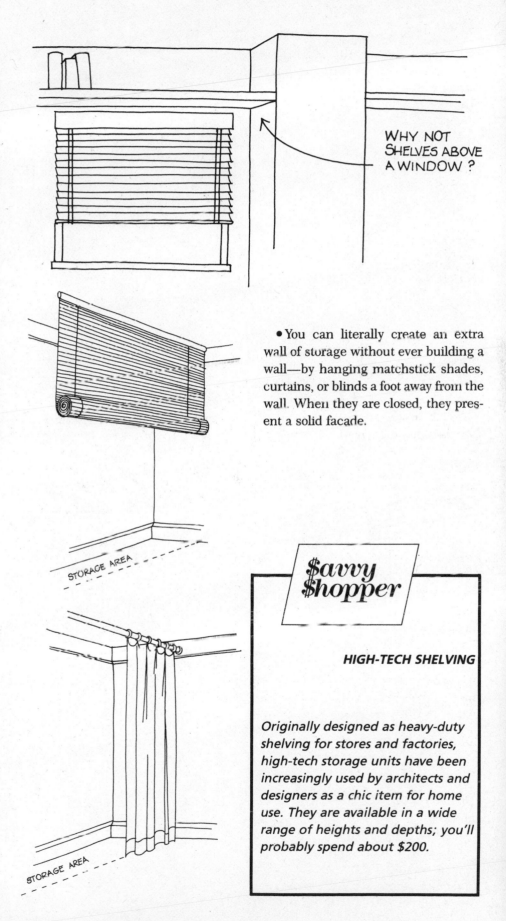

WHY NOT SHELVES ABOVE A WINDOW?

STORAGE AREA

STORAGE AREA

• You can literally create an extra wall of storage without ever building a wall—by hanging matchstick shades, curtains, or blinds a foot away from the wall. When they are closed, they present a solid facade.

CREATING EXTRA SPACE

There are as many creative solutions to finding extra storage space as there are people looking for ideas. You have to start with the belief that there *is* a way to solve the problem if you think about it long enough. It may be in "creating" a new wall, or using space and furniture more cleverly. Good luck!

• Formica chests, which cost about $120, are a great buy. These chests are generally part of a series in which one can add stacking units, storage drawers, and bookshelves to create a whole storage wall.

$avvy $hopper

HIGH-TECH SHELVING

Originally designed as heavy-duty shelving for stores and factories, high-tech storage units have been increasingly used by architects and designers as a chic item for home use. They are available in a wide range of heights and depths; you'll probably spend about $200.

• Use chests with drawers as end tables. You can also make your coffee table serve double-duty by using a chest that opens on top.

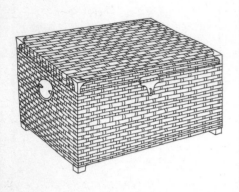

• The space in front of the convector can be invaluable for storage. Build in shelving to hide the convector and also provide storage and seating space.
• Every surface of the apartment offers a possible area for storage: consider using the bottoms of cabinets and backs of doors for storage. In the layout below, one piece of furniture serves multiple uses, epitomizing the clever use of storage space.

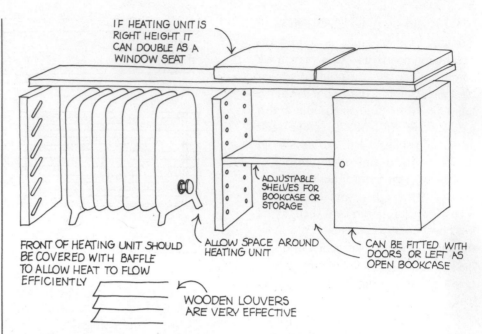

IF HEATING UNIT IS RIGHT HEIGHT IT CAN DOUBLE AS A WINDOW SEAT

ADJUSTABLE SHELVES FOR BOOKCASE OR STORAGE

FRONT OF HEATING UNIT SHOULD BE COVERED WITH BAFFLE TO ALLOW HEAT TO FLOW EFFICIENTLY

ALLOW SPACE AROUND HEATING UNIT

CAN BE FITTED WITH DOORS OR LEFT AS OPEN BOOKCASE

WOODEN LOUVERS ARE VERY EFFECTIVE

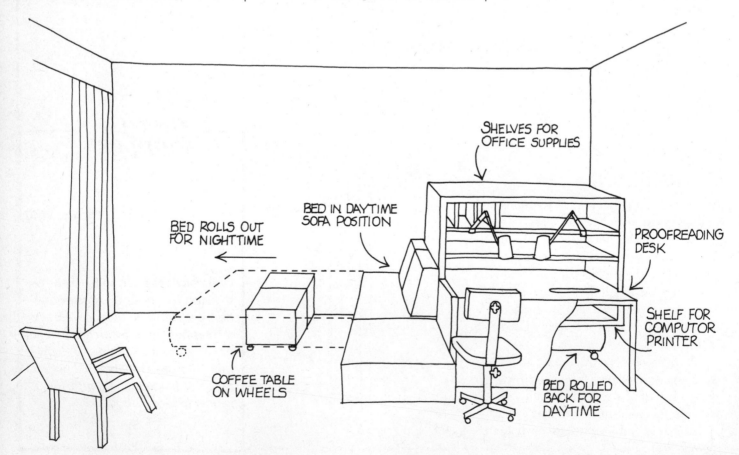

SHELVES FOR OFFICE SUPPLIES

BED IN DAYTIME SOFA POSITION

BED ROLLS OUT FOR NIGHTTIME

PROOFREADING DESK

SHELF FOR COMPUTOR PRINTER

COFFEE TABLE ON WHEELS

BED ROLLED BACK FOR DAYTIME

DECORATING DILEMMA

Working at Home

Elinor Jacobs is a freelance illustrator whose office is at home. She needs enough space to store her portfolios, designs, swatch cards, and customer files. "It wouldn't seem like such a problem if I didn't also need a large bulletin board. I like to put my drawings up and then step back from them. There isn't an extra wall in the apartment where I can install a bulletin board. And if the board is put above the desk, then I lose the one area where I can store books."

DESIGNERS: PAUL SHAFER AND JEAN WEINER

Although Elinor was concerned about not having enough space along the 10-foot wall for storage and display, the solution was relatively simple and straightforward. We built in bookshelves across the long wall and installed two sliding doors with a cork finish so she could use pushpins to hang her drawings. Under the shelf, we installed shelves for pencils and notepads.

Elinor had one more area she hadn't noticed. Between the pillar and the window, there was a 2-foot space that could be used for bookshelves without crowding her work area.

Two filing cabinets were squeezed into a space that was, theoretically, only large enough for one and a half. This was accomplished by turning one sideways and placing it on casters so that it slides out easily.

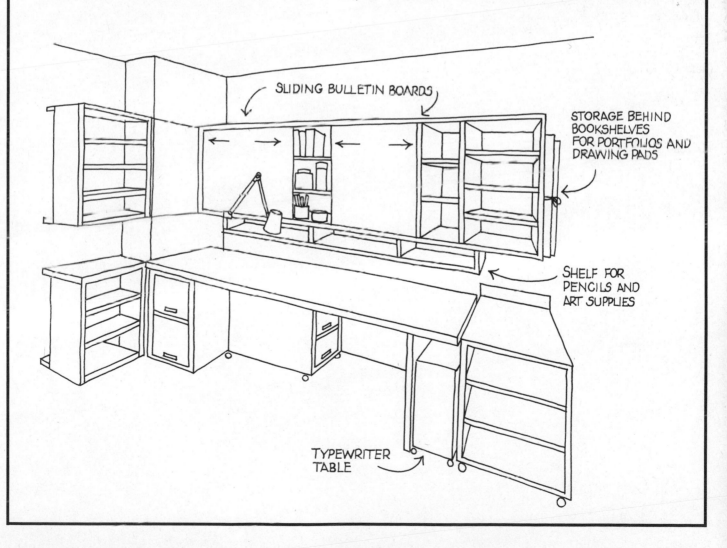

AFTERWORD

You've come a long way. You've worked with ten of New York's top designers and seen the way they approach decorating problems similar to yours. I'm sure that you enjoyed the learning process and that you'll now do a wonderful job with your own place.

I hope that for years to come you'll use this as a handbook and refer to it time and again. We all wish you great happiness in your first apartment—and all your future homes.

Karen Fisher

INDEX

DECORATOR PROFILES

RONALD BRICKE is noted for his wizardry in using traditional furniture to create light, airy, and memorable rooms. He is particularly known for his attention to detail and handsome renovations which turn the most mundane rooms into unique spaces. In 1972, he opened his own firm (Ronald Bricke & Associates), designing residential and commercial spaces.

COBUILD is a New York design firm founded in 1980 by partners PAUL SHAFER and JEAN WEINER. They specialize in space planning, treating every square inch of an apartment as though it were a jewel to be lovingly treasured and well used.

KIM FREEMAN has been the Decorating Editor for both *House Beautiful* and *Mademoiselle*. She is currently a freelance stylist with her credit line appearing regularly in such publications as the New York Times.

STANLEY HURA uses his dramatic and elegant decorating ideas in styling the J.P. Stevens model rooms, which are regularly seen in such magazines as *Ladies Home Journal*, *Cosmopolitan*, and *Women's Day*.

HOWARD KAPLAN is one of the most knowledgeable figures in French Country furniture and decor. He designs furniture, pottery and lamps, and textiles and wall paper for his French Country stores throughout the nation.

GERALD KUHN established his own company (Gerald Kuhn, Inc.) in 1979. Known parimarily for architectural interior renovations, he specializes in residential and office design. He designs powerful spaces by using simple color schemes and layouts which serve as dramatic backgrounds for carefully chosen artwork and sculpture.

RICHARD KNAPPLE is famous for the model rooms that he plans for Bloomingdale's in New York, where he is Vice President of Interior Design. He travels regularly to Europe and the Far East in search of ideas and inspiration.

LYNN LEVENBERG is a former Decorating Editor of *American Home* magazine and currently president of her own company (Lynn Levenberg Interiors, Inc.). She decorates residences and offices in New York, including the offices of *Cosmopolitan*. A long-standing devotee of English design, she employs the gracious colors, patterns, and furnishings of a London drawing room in even the most typical New York high rise apartments.

TIM MEIER is Second Vice President of Design Construction/Branch Administration for Smith Barney. He is an architect as well as a designer and his experience in designing offices across the country gives him a uniquely practical approach to decorating.

ABOUT THE AUTHOR

KAREN FISHER is a central figure in the decorating world. She is the president of Decorator Previews, which represents more than fifty of New York's leading interior designers. Prior to founding Decorator Previews, Karen was the decorating editor for *Cosmopolitan*, the style editor for *Esquire*, and the executive editor for *American Home*. She's also written many other decorating books, including *Living for Today* (Viking), *The Power Look at Home* (Morrow), and *Quick Fix Decorating Ideas* (New American Library).

ABOUT
THE
ILLUSTRATOR

Before devoting his talents full time to illustration, PAUL WOLLMAN enjoyed a successful career as an Art Director in several top Advertising Agencies. He won numerous awards creating not only on Madison Avenue, but also in Paris, London, and Dusseldorf. His illustrations—from magazine covers to editorial illustrations—have appeared nationally.

He was educated at Pratt Institute and divides his time between New York and Marbella. Paul Wollman and his wife Anne have two children.